Profiling Your Date

Profiling Your Date

A SMART WOMAN'S GUIDE
TO EVALUATING A MAN

Dr. Caroline Presno, Ed.D., P.C.C.

 St. Martin's Griffin ❧ *New York*

title page art from veer

www.stmartins.com

Book design by Judith Stagnitto Abbate/Abbate Design

Kind permission has been granted to reprint from the following:

American Psychiatric Association. *Diagnostic and Statistical Manual of Mental Disorders*, Third Edition, Revised. Washington, DC: American Psychiatric Association, 1987.

American Psychiatric Association. *Diagnostic and Statistical Manual of Mental Disorders*, Fourth Edition, Text Revision. Washington, DC: American Psychiatric Association, 2000.

Excerpt from the American Society of Addiction Medicine, Public Policy Statement on the Definition of Alcoholism (adopted September 1976, revised February 1990). Copyright © 2005, American Society of Addiction Medicine. The full statement may be accessed at www.ASAM.org.

Library of Congress Cataloging-in-Publication Data

Presno, Caroline.
    Profiling your date : a smart woman's guide to evaluating a man / Caroline Presno.—1st ed.
       p. cm.
    Includes bibliographical references and index.
    ISBN-13: 978-0-312-36227-0
    ISBN-10: 0-312-36227-7
  1. Mate selection.   2. Man-woman relationships.   I. Title.

HQ801.P888   2007
646.7'7—dc22

                                              2007017428

First St. Martin's Griffin Edition: September 2007

10 9 8 7 6 5 4 3 2 1

For my father,
Dr. Vincent Presno

Contents

Acknowledgments

I WOULD LIKE TO acknowledge my editor, Sheila Curry Oakes, who believed in this book, supported it, and through the editing process, enhanced the manuscript. There is nothing like working with someone when you're both on the same page.

Many thanks to my literary agent, Mollie Glick at the Jean V. Naggar Literary Agency, for finding a home for *Profiling Your Date*. Mollie has a keen knowledge of the publishing world, was always there for me, and knows how to ease a writer's anxiety!

I want to express appreciation to all my friends whose enthusiasm, wonderful insights, and compelling relationship stories helped make *Profiling Your Date* the book that it is—with particular thanks to Dr. Marcy Gunn. Much gratitude also to Jennifer Melke, Dr. David and Cindy Klosterman, Drs. Bob and Beverly Weisman, Carolyn Thomas, Nicole Gianuglou, Kimberly Kmentt, Germaine Valentine, Donna DeFabritus, Mary Ritter, Martha Kiser, and Joe McNamara.

A poignant thank-you is reserved for my late father, Dr. Vincent Presno. He was a writer, a professor, and a man who showed me that Mr. Self-Actualized really does exist. Of course, my mother, Carol Presno, who is Ms. Self-Actualized, was the perfect match for him.

During the book-writing process, my mother has been part care-taker, part idea generator, and part role model as a woman who is so lovely and at ease with herself.

To my love, Don Baker: You've been profiled!—as warm, wonder-ful, and my perfect match. And isn't it fantastic for me that "the one" is a journalist. Thank you, Don, for your curiosity and creativity, which makes every day fun. But most of all, thank you for being so loving.

Last but not least, thanks to the many, many men who have dated me—yes, that means you! Without all the guys, I would have had no one to profile—how dull life would have been without you!

Foreword

I AM PLEASED TO HAVE the opportunity to tell you a little about Caroline Presno, Ed.D., P.C.C., and her exciting book, *Profiling Your Date: A Smart Woman's Guide to Evaluating a Man*.

I have known Dr. Caroline Presno for more than twenty years, and I can tell you she brings her intelligence, innovation, and perceptiveness into writing this book. Dr. Caroline's profiling technique combines a commonsense approach with an understanding of established psychological principles and of pertinent research findings. She helps the average dating woman fine-tune her radar, to home in on an ideal partner.

As her friend, as well as being a licensed clinical psychologist and a thirty-something single woman searching for my own Mr. Right, I fully appreciate the value of Dr. Caroline's work. The dating world is filled with many emotional pitfalls and, at times, physical dangers. Her profiling technique—and the information she provides about various personality and emotional issues to watch for in potential dates—arms the single woman with more insight into her own needs and goals, as well as teaches her skills to better cultivate the relationships that match and to quickly weed out the mismatches.

Dr. Caroline begins by guiding you through the use of communication techniques that can speed up the initial process of gaining personal knowledge about a date and can enhance the quality of the relationship over time. She then helps you to develop your own unique profile of what you are looking for in a dating partner.

Next, Dr. Caroline offers crucial information that helps the reader differentiate between normal personality traits and minor and/or tolerable personality quirks versus signs of a man with a serious pathology. She covers the span from everyday emotional issues, such as situational depression and anxiety, to the deeply ingrained personality disorders and other pathologies that the sensible woman wants to steer far clear of.

Dr. Caroline also touches on other timely and crucial factors about which to maintain an awareness during the dating process, such as sexually transmitted diseases, tendencies toward violence, and addictions. Additionally, she addresses the tremendous recent shift in how potential partners meet, such as online and at speed-dating gatherings.

Caroline Presno's profiling technique provides a deeper, more informative approach than the typical dating how-to book. Yet she also presents it in an accessible and concise manner that does the work for you, the reader, of plodding through psychological and sociological research and psychiatric diagnostic manuals. In conclusion, I expect that as it is for me, *Profiling Your Date: A Smart Woman's Guide to Evaluating a Man* will become your indispensable dating guide.

MARCY J. GUNN, PSY.D.
Clinical Psychologist
Antoinette S. Cordell, Ph.D.,
and Associates, LLC

Profiling Your Date

Empower Yourself Through Profiling

PROFILING IS THE ONLY WAY to date. Nothing else is more empowering. Nothing else is more effective. Nothing else is more fun. *Profiling Your Date* is how I have dated; it's how I live; and it's how I found the love of my life. Even though men frustrated me at times, I loved them and couldn't stay away. I never gave up.

Profiling my dates has been a joy because it has allowed me to get to know the testosterone-ridden human being next to me. In writing this book, I wanted to provide a mix of fun and entertainment together with serious relationship information for serious relationship decisions. Date profiling is a unique and effective way of learning about a man in-depth and, if you choose, establishing an intimate connection with him.

I am a psychotherapist (P.C.C.), an educator (Ed.D.), and someone who knows dating. Through my personal and professional experience I have developed an approach to dating that will help you gain quick and easy insight into each of your dates to determine if he's the one for you.

Aside from the sources cited throughout *Profiling Your Date*, you'll also notice hypotheses based on experiences, as well as examples that highlight these experiences. The examples I use in this book are based on real-world themes but not on real people. In many cases, you'll find that either you or someone you know has gone through situations similar to the ones presented in this book.

Of course, every woman who dates tries to understand the man she's with. It's natural. People habitually perceive, judge, analyze, classify, and sometimes criticize. However, it's possible to create a more objective picture by using the tools and techniques of psychology and counseling theory. Now we can call on expert advice and research to add to our understanding of a man. By psychologically profiling the men we date, our perceptions become crisper, our judgments more accurate, our analyses wiser, and our classifications increasingly well defined.

Think Like a Therapist

THIS BOOK IS FOR all the smart women out there who want to draw on psychological information and are tired of silly dating strategies. *Profiling Your Date* gives you the kind of information you'd get if you were listening to a group of off-the-clock single psychotherapists chatting with their coworkers about last night's dates. This book gives you the information we in the field have, so that you can apply it to your own dating experiences.

I will give you a combination of clinical experience, personal experience, psychological theory and method, and research study results.

What Is Profiling?

PROFILING A MAN is a two-part process: The first part is getting to know the guy, and the second part is seeing if he's right for you. As you'll notice, the first part of profiling—getting to know him—is more objective than the second part, which is very subjective and personal.

GETTING TO KNOW THE GUY

Profiling a man means developing a breadth and depth of knowledge of his thoughts, feelings, and behaviors. It allows you to understand him and be able to grasp his perspective of the world and of relationships in particular. It's finding out what makes him tick.

You have the exciting task of sketching out a meaningful personality profile that accurately reflects the chosen man and shows your understanding of him. How many times have you woken out of a dead sleep with burning questions about someone you're seeing? Don't you just want to *know*—know why he's treating you this way, what he's thinking, and where he's coming from?

Profiling is a systematic process that allows you to develop the understanding that you crave. In this book, you'll discover explicit techniques to get him to open up, specific things to watch for in conversation and behavior, and what these things might mean.

You'll learn systematic ways to profile for:

- his degree of commitment readiness
- his aptitude for intimacy
- his likelihood of being a stalker, rapist, or abusive partner
- his chance of lying, being unfaithful, or carrying an STD
- his tendency toward big, bad personality problems like narcissism, paranoia, and sociopathy
- his moods
- his level of anxiety
- his wonderful qualities like warmth, authenticity, and openness
- his potential for fulfilling his potential

DETERMININE IF HE'S RIGHT FOR YOU

As you begin to have some sense of who he is, you are also figuring out if he's right for you. You're profiling to see if you fit together well.

At different points in the relationship, the question "Is he right for me?" can take on different meanings. The following relationship dilemmas are liable to kick your profiling skills into high gear:

- Do I want to go on a first date with him?
- What about the chemistry? Is there enough spark potential between us?
- How many dates should I give this before I cut it off?
- Should we break up or make up?
- Should I live with him?
- Should we get married?

As you learn new and more intimate things about this man over time, you'll go through the process of evaluating and reevaluating his rightness for you.

WHAT PROFILING CAN'T DO

Profiling Your Date is intended to be a down-and-dirty overview, not a comprehensive diagnostic or treatment guide. For that, you need to check into other sources. The list of references in the Notes section at the conclusion of this book should be a help to you. If you are looking for diagnosis and treatment, there is no substitute for you or your date consulting with a mental-health professional.

How Can Profiling Benefit Me?

THERE ARE SPECIFIC WAYS you can benefit from the profiling process.

PROFILING GIVES YOU AN INTENSITY OF UNDERSTANDING THAT WILL IMPRESS HIM

Profiling gives you depth of insight into his beliefs and behaviors that will blow him away. With incisive understanding, you'll break through his social veneer and get in touch with who he really is. And he will love it!

He will love it because he'll sense your interest in getting to know him and your growing awareness of who he is. As discussed in Chapter 2, "Getting into His Head and into His Heart," one of a man's greatest desires is to be understood by a woman. A feeling of empathy and warmth will wash over him as you gain understanding of him though profiling.

While profiling may sound as if it is intrusive, abrasive, and lacking in emotion, it is not. When you do it right, profiling is subtle and insinuating. There's delicacy in listening to and interpreting a man's words. There's grace in reading his body language. There's beauty in psychological awareness of another human being. You are not becoming an amateur therapist and analyzing every thought, word, or deed. You are fine-tuning your awareness of him so you can connect beyond a superficial level.

You have the opportunity to establish a connection between yourself and the man you choose. You can distinguish yourself by connecting with him at a deeper level. This doesn't necessarily mean that you have to talk to him about "deep" topics like life and death on the first date. The connection can start small—acknowledging that you get certain things about him. Over time, he'll notice not only that you're getting the small stuff but that you're perceptive enough to develop the big picture about him as well.

Where the connection you develop will lead is hard to say. For a romance to develop, there has to be more than understanding. You may find that you get him and can't stand what he's about. He also may not be making the attempt to understand you; however, this won't happen often.

In many cases you'll find that the connection you've established leads to a fantastic friendship or a wonderful relationship. As your relationship develops, don't stop the profiling, because it played some part in getting you to your current situation and can help maintain the understanding in your relationship.

PROFILING GIVES YOU COURAGE

Profiling gives you the courage to say, "Next!" which is not always easy. It can be an extremely gut-wrenching decision to pass on a guy, particularly if he's interested in you. There are pressures to couple up, and we have to deal with our feelings of loneliness and the very natural desire to share a life with someone.

Because profiling makes dating much clearer, you'll become more and more confident in your decision-making skills. When the unpleasant truth is staring you down, you'll rise to the challenge and muster the courage to make the appropriate decision. Being miserable with a man isn't an option, whether it's the first date or the first-year anniversary. Profiling brings clarity to your situation so you have to deal with it. Rather than settling for less than what you want, you will have the confidence to try again with someone else.

Happily, profiling also highlights goodness and can give you the courage to take a chance on a man. Due to bad experiences in the past, you may be overlooking some men with wonderful qualities. Or you may be just plain scared to grow the relationship beyond a certain point. Profiling sheds light on both of you so that you can move forward in a positive direction. It takes a lot of courage to take a chance on someone.

Last but not least, profiling builds your confidence so that you are less intimidated and more apt to try today's new dating venues.

Along with the old standbys like pubs and clubs, there are Internet and speed-dating events. Communities are also seeing the need to cater to singles. More and more church groups for singles are popping up, as well as neighborhood organizations and clubs designed to get people mingling.

Today, many men and women are remaining single. A survey from the University of Chicago found that on average, typical city dwellers are going to be single for half of their lives.[1] That's a big change from previous generations.

According to U.S. Census Bureau statistics, there are 95.7 million singles in this country.[2] That means 43 percent of U.S. residents age fifteen and over are unmarried and single.

You are not alone, and profiling is a tool to help you find the courage to go out and start dating for a mate.

PROFILING LETS YOU SQUEEZE THE PRODUCE

Psychiatrist Dr. Alice Onady uses a fun analogy to describe the dating process.[3] She likens it to being a cabbage on the produce shelf that is going to be squeezed, thumped, and either chosen or rejected. She maintains that in relationships, *you* want to be the one assessing the produce. At all costs, you should avoid being the cabbage that gets picked up, sniffed, squeezed, and thrown back. How do you avoid this fate? Through profiling, of course, because it allows you to be the one making the assessment.

In essence, Dr. Onady is saying that you want to be empowered in your dealings with men. Forget lying there like a passive cabbage, handing him all the power. Recognize the amount of control you have. Profile him and look at who he is and decide if that's what *you* want!

There is no reason to go on a date worrying excessively about whether he likes you or not. Have the attitude that you are going out to see if you like him. This makes dating and relationships so much less nerve-racking and so much easier on your self-esteem.

This is not to say that he has no input in this relationship. Just like you, he is going to be looking at who you are and if you're right for him. That's okay. However, there is simply no reason to completely turn over the reins and let yourself get oversqueezed and picked apart.

Over the years, there may have been a number of things you blamed yourself for that may have had more to do with him than you thought. For example, Chapter 8, "Date with a Narcissist," is about the narcissistic man who loves no one but himself. In all likelihood, if you dated such a man, you became very self-critical when this guy didn't show an interest in you. Maybe you thought you weren't attractive enough or smart enough, when the reality was he wasn't emotionally healthy enough to establish and maintain a relationship.

Profiling helps you see that with some men, what you look like, what you say, or the way you act have little to do with how much they like you or not. With these types, their own mental health issues are the driving force in what keeps the relationship from getting off the ground, not anything you do or say.

You can stand on your head and sing an opera, but a sociopathic man will always be manipulative. You can hop on one foot and plead for trust, but a paranoid man will always be jealous and suspicious. By squeezing the cabbage in the right way, you'll be able to tell if you're dating this type of pathologically driven man.

When your cabbage squeezing has helped you discover a relatively healthy man, profiling helps you examine your role in the relationship from a more objective perspective, encouraging self-examination and constructive self-critique.

Profiling doesn't seek to blame and shame men. It's simply that we want to put our energy and work into a relationship in which there is a chance of a good payoff. Why waste time getting upset over a man who's not worth getting upset over? Instead, it's much better to move down the produce aisle!

PROFILING HELPS KEEP YOU SAFE

While growing up, the rule was not to talk to strangers. But dating inevitably involves talking to someone you don't really know. You may find yourself sharing a meal with some guy who seemingly dropped from the sky or, in worse circumstances, crawled out from under a rock!

If you were to ask your friends, you would discover that many have gone out with a man not knowing his family, friends, or much else other than his name and job. The unknown can be exciting but also scary.

There's no guarantee that if the guy comes with "references" from friends or family he will be without problems or issues. It's easy to get lulled into a false sense of security. "Well, if he's Mom's cousin's friend, of course he has got to be a safe date!" Not necessarily. The more contextual information the better, but in essence, Mom's cousin's friend is still a stranger to you.

Admittedly, it's uncomfortable to think about all the horrible things that could happen when you go out with a man. Dating shouldn't be about dread and fear. It should be about fun and romance.

Unfortunately, we have to look out for ourselves. We can count on friends and loved ones, but at the end of the day, we must value ourselves enough to take charge of our own safety. This means being conscious of what can happen to us and facing that fear by taking the appropriate actions.

In his book *The Gift of Fear*, Gavin De Becker talks about the importance of listening to fear and protecting yourself by systematically evaluating a man. He emphasizes: "The whole process is most similar to an audition, except that the stakes are higher. A date might look like the audition in *Tootsie*, in which the man wants the part so badly that he'll do anything to get it, or it can be an opportunity for the woman to evaluate important pre-incident indicators. Doesn't sound romantic? Well, daters are doing an evaluation anyway; they're just doing it badly. I am suggesting only that the evaluation be conscious and informed."[4]

Although dating need not be fear driven, we do need to incorporate the potential for danger in our conception of the dating process, along with hearts and chocolate. It's just smart to be safe.

After the initial shock of having to think about the dangers of dating wears off, you'll find that your anxiety level decreases over time with profiling. It won't plunge to zero and it shouldn't, because having some anxiety serves as a protective function during relationship building. It motivates us to guard ourselves and alerts us to possible danger.

With profiling you should maintain a healthy level of fear, because you're taking care of business, but you're not letting fear get in the way of meeting people. You're doing all you can to protect yourself, so there's no need to obsess. Profiling lets you recognize the clues you need to weed out the scary dates, and gives you safety tips to use with every guy, just in case.

PROFILING MAKES YOU NATURALLY HARD TO GET

A pleasant side effect of the profiling process is that you become naturally hard to get through your selectivity. Being naturally hard to get versus playing or acting hard to get are two completely different scenarios. For one thing, acting aloof and uninterested never really works. Men instinctively sniff out the act and treat you accordingly.

On the other hand, truly being hard to get carries some weight. With profiling, you get some objectivity and perspective that cause you to stand back a bit. You're not being cold but are maintaining a warm independence.

With profiling, there is no need to play the head games that are supposed to make a man think the woman is indifferent. If you're interested in him, the authentic and spontaneous thing to do is to let it show in your own natural way. You can return his phone calls. You can tell him what a nice time you had. Profiling allows you to be your genuine self while at the same time helps you maintain your autonomy.

If you're not desperate and needy there is simply no reason to worry about appearing desperate and needy, because you won't. Let other women waste their time, energy, and IQ on rude games. It's time to throw out the old rules and make way for profiling!

PROFILING IS YOUR CRYSTAL BALL TO HIS BEHAVIOR

Once you have a good understanding of his past and current behavior, you have a better chance of predicting his future behavior. In statistical terms, when one variable forecasts another, it's called predictive validity.

It's like having a crystal ball that gives you glimpses into the future. You can get an idea of whether or not this guy has long-term potential. You can get a preview of what your lifestyle with him will be like. Not to mention how he will treat you, your family, and any future children.

Imagine the luxury of knowing what he's going to do ahead of time—and maybe before he knows it himself. Understanding what sets him off, as well as what gets him off, gives you more to work with in the relationship. You won't get blindsided by a creep in sheep's clothing.

The great thing about predictive validity is that you can test for it. Using the information you've gathered from profiling after you read this book, go ahead and make some educated guesses about his behavior and keep them in mind. For instance, you can try predicting when he will call next or how long it will be before he's ready to be exclusive. You can also hypothesize how he will react to certain situations, both emotionally and behaviorally.

You can also make predictions about your friends' relationships, celeb hookups, and reality TV show romances. No matter what you're making predictions about, be sure to keep tabs on accuracy. The more you practice and the more you profile, the more you'll find you're right!

Past behavior foreshadows future behavior. Want to know what he is going to do now or ten years from now? Look at what he did in the past. Has he cheated before? There's a good chance he'll do it again. Has he been very controlling with you in the past? Most likely he will be controlling with you in the future. Has he consistently treated you with respect over time? Looks like he'll probably always treat you with respect.

Of course you don't want to go overboard. It's important to leave some room for change. It does happen—for good and for bad. However, nobody wants to be stuck wishing, waiting, and hoping for positive change for too long. With accurate predictions, you won't.

One last cautionary note: Don't turn your predictions into self-fulfilling prophecies. The danger here is that you may unconsciously start to make the prediction come true. For example, if you predict that your relationship won't last past two months, then you might actually contribute to the destruction of the relationship without being aware of it.

Keep the predictions objective and in perspective. They're

probabilities, not certainties. And after all, pleasant surprises in relationships can come out of left field.

PROFILING PROMOTES LOOKING BEFORE YOU LEAP

A few women might say, "Stepping back and being partly objective stinks! I'm an emotional, spontaneous person who would rather dive in headfirst as long as it feels right." Profiling gives you the advantages of looking before you leap rather than leaping before you look. The best strategy for women who have the habit of plunging into relationships is to contemplate the negative consequences that come from bad choices:

- Have you ever slept with a seemingly caring man only to find a cool stranger next to you a few weeks later? How did it feel?
- How would you react to being swept off your feet by a tirelessly attentive man who turns into a dangerous stalker? Has it happened to you?
- Have you ever thought you were in love, made the announcement to everyone you know, and practically set the date, only to realize it wasn't really love? What would it be like to go through that more than once?
- How do you feel after wasting time and energy on a man who isn't for you? Drained? Discouraged? Disappointed? Cheated?

For the purpose of evaluating a man, you need to maintain some initial distance so that you can be objective and truthful with yourself about his fabulous qualities as well as his flaws. Becoming physically intimate too quickly, pouring out your soul after the movie, picking out the wedding dress, and other ways of forcing him into your life prematurely render you impotent in terms of profiling.

In the end, a little remoteness born out of the profiling process can help you avoid some of the more disastrous consequences of relationships, so you can better experience all the joyful things that make being with a man wonderful. You don't have to throw out all the spontaneity and emotional energy. Profiling simply helps you to channel that energy in the right direction so that you don't waste it.

POWER IS KNOWLEDGE; PROFILING IS POWER!

Having information, seeing things, knowing things is power! Ignorance really isn't bliss. Ignorance or hiding from the truth can sneak up on people awfully quickly and with dire consequences. At some point, every one of us has chosen to look the other way when she wasn't seeing what she wanted to see.

What woman hasn't ignored warning signs about a guy because she wanted him to be "the one"? Women often try to wish a frog into a prince by running from the truth of what they know or choose not to know. At what cost? We all pay for the sham bliss of ignorance down the line.

Go ahead and claim your power! You'll be happy that you did. Think of people you know or are familiar with who have achieved some success in life. They were informed and knowledgeable about their area of expertise. They watched people, understood human interaction, and were psychologically aware. They faced the truth—good or bad—and dealt with it.

PROFILING IS FUN!

Profiling simply makes dating more fun—particularly if you're on the fence about the dating process. It is fun because it takes a lot of the pressure off of you. The emphasis is getting to know the man you're with, which enables you to take the focus off of your insecurities. When you go into the date with more confidence, you almost automatically have more fun.

It's entertaining to get to know a man this way. It's a richer experience filled with the amusing nuances of human behavior. Go out, profile, and have fun!

A word of caution: The profiling process isn't meant to make a man feel as if he's being grilled or investigated. Yes, profiling is in many ways pragmatic. However, the date profiler cannot sacrifice beauty, joy, and passion to pragmatism. That sucks the fun out of life.

Profiling or developing an understanding of someone and how that someone fits with you should have an elegant flow and natural feel. If at any time it turns into an obsessive point-by-point evaluation, dial it down!

2

Getting into His Head and into His Heart

HOW DO YOU GET into a man's head? How can you move toward *really* knowing him? For years, psychotherapists have cultivated different techniques and tricks of the trade that encourage people to talk openly. Most people don't automatically come into a therapy session and spill their guts. It takes effort and skill to get someone to converse candidly. Because men tend to be more reticent than women when it comes to sharing thoughts and expressing feelings, they often require a bit more finesse.

The key element here is that although men may not be as forthcoming, they still want to be understood! Through the process of profiling, you can give this feeling to a man because the essence of profiling is understanding. If you understand the mind, you can seduce the heart.

Not only will you develop more understanding by using these therapy techniques, but you will also greatly improve the quality and flow of your conversations with men. Have you ever been in a situation where even the best conversation starters sink like a lead balloon? Armed with these therapy techniques, you'll find it so much easier to get the lead out!

Therapy 101

THE PSYCHOLOGIST CARL RODGERS detailed three main conditions for a successful therapeutic experience and healthy human development.[1] If you can create these conditions, at least in part, on a date, you'll have a man on your hands who opens up like a flower in spring. These techniques are so powerful and so effective in the advancement of human relationships that you'll more than likely be floored by the results. These three conditions are empathy, unconditional positive regard, and congruence.

EMPATHY

Empathizing with a man allows you to penetrate the wall that separates you from his thoughts and feelings. It's the act of putting yourself in his shoes and trying to see the world from his perspective. This process of making meaning out of a man's words so that you can grasp his subjective experience of the world is both profound and moving. As you feel this special connection, he will feel it.

Of course, you're never going to be able to understand what he's going through completely, fully, 100 percent. That would be boring, anyway. It would take the mystery out of everything. Psychotherapists never assume, "Oh, yes, I know exactly what it's like to be you right now." They try to get an idea or an approximation of what the client experiences at any given moment.

To do this, psychotherapists draw on thoughts and feelings that are common to humanity. We all experience confusion, emptiness, joy, and hope. Even if it's not possible to relate to a specific event, it is possible to relate to some of the emotions and ideas behind it. For instance, a man might share a story about a football game he played and lost. It doesn't matter if you have never played football. Try drawing on another experience that will help you connect with his

sense of loss. It could be something as similar as a soccer defeat or
something as seemingly different as losing the lead in a play to a rival.

When you empathize with a man, it's not enough to hold it inside. You must convey your empathy to him so that he can appreciate it. Nonverbal expressions such as a touch on the hand, a wrinkle of the brow, or a poignant, lingering gaze all can let this man know that you understand and are in his corner.

One of the most common verbal techniques that therapists use to convey empathy is paraphrasing. If you haven't tried it, you won't believe how well it works! Paraphrasing can be more effective than simply questioning for the purpose of getting him to talk to you, because it's subtle yet penetrating. When you paraphrase, you are making sense out of what he has just said, summarizing it, and then repeating it back to him in your own words.

What makes paraphrasing more than just a plain summary is that you are getting at the real meaning of what he is saying.[2] It's as if you are building onto a foundation he has already laid out for you. Better yet, you are digging underneath the foundation to find out what unknowns are buried there. Through paraphrasing, you are creating new insights, both for you and for him. Take a look at the following example:

1 Logan: I've been head of the marketing division about two years

2 now. Working for a private defense company is so different from my

3 government job.

4 Charlotte: How is it different?

5 Logan: The pay. I mean the pay, it's more than double. It's like they

6 throw money at you in bonuses. And I've traveled to more cities in the

7 last two years than I've ever been to in my life. You name it, from

8 Seattle to DC (*laughs*). Sometimes I don't know whether I'm in the sky

9 or on the ground.

10 **Charlotte: From what you're saying, there are some great benefits to your**

11 **job. It seems like you find the travel pretty exciting, but also kind of**

12 **tiring (*great paraphrasing*).**

13 Logan: Yeah, lately it's like I'm going to a new place every week. Last

14 month, I got back on a Sunday night from visiting my parents for the

15 holidays—and I got back late, too, because of weather delay after

16 delay. Anyway, I got my messages and it's, "You're leaving for Dallas

17 Monday morning; the flight's at 8 A.M." Damn, I wanted to say, "Forget

18 it," but I can't, you know? People are getting laid off left and right, and

19 you've got to pull your weight. It's about one person doing the work of

20 two or three people.

21 **Charlotte: So they didn't give you notice or prep time for what sounded**

22 **like an important meeting. And besides that, you didn't have the**

23 **option of saying no. That must have made you feel more than a little**

24 **annoyed and maybe even kind of trapped (*more great paraphrasing*).**

25 Logan: "Totally, trapped . . . yeah, that's how I feel, trapped. The money and

26 opportunity for promotion hook you, but they make you pay for it in

27 blood. It's been a problem for me in other relationships because this job

28 sneaks up on you and takes over (*pause*) . . . Lately, I've been

29 thinking about leaving it, but really, where do I go? Back to school?

30 What?

Through empathic understanding, Charlotte was able to draw out his true feelings about the job. Notice that Logan started out almost boasting (perhaps to impress her) about his job, yet by the end of the conversation, he reveals that discontent is causing him to think about other options. Also, the information Charlotte got about this job causing problems in past relationships was especially pertinent to her.

Because Charlotte senses more than meets the eye in his first statement, she starts off with an open question that causes him to expand on the old job verses the new job (line 4). Then in lines 10–12, Charlotte begins to empathize by summarizing his thoughts and emotions, which serves to help him clarify things. She hits the nail on the head by bringing his feeling of "tiredness" to the forefront (lines 11–12).

Logan validates that Charlotte is right (line 13) by agreeing with her and then discussing the topic in further detail. In the event that Charlotte misinterpreted, Logan would have corrected her by saying something such as, "Well, not exactly" or "Not really, I feel more like . . ."

Finally, Charlotte brings it all home by capturing the fact the Logan feels "trapped," which is an excellent word choice in this case. Thus, by repeating his thoughts and emotions in different, more incisive words, Charlotte is able to elicit a deeper and more authentic set of thoughts and emotions than those with which the conversation began. She should continue in the same vein to find out more about his future plans.

In case the cat has got your tongue, read over these lists of empathic words and phrases and store them away for your next date.

It Sounds Like You Felt . . .

accepted	awesome	defiant	embarrassed
adventurous	awful	depressed	empty
alone	comfortable	devastated	encouraged
annoyed	confused	disappointed	excited
anxious	cursed	drained	freaked
fried	liked	panicky	screwed
frustrated	lost	peaceful	sick

fulfilled	lousy	playful	shocked
great	loved	poetic	terrified
happy	low	proud	toasted
hard up	lucky	punked	upset
hurt	nauseous	ready	weird
intrigued	on top of it	sad	whipped
kidlike	oppressed	satisfied	

THAT SITUATION MUST HAVE . . .

been hellish	left you cold
been incredible	pleased you
been worthwhile	put you on the defensive
blown your mind	rattled you
caught you by surprise	rocked you
changed you	seemed hopeless
enlightened you	seemed surreal
freaked you out	strengthened you
given you great memories	taken you off guard

NO CONDITIONS!

Unconditional positive regard means that you value and accept a person as he or she is without exception. It seems like a simple enough concept, but in practice it's very tough to achieve. How often can you say that you have fully accepted another person without conditions? How many people in your life have accepted you unconditionally? For most people, the list is probably small. One of the primary reasons people connect with a therapist is that therapists can give them the unconditional positive regard that may be lacking in their lives.

Some lucky children are raised with unconditional love. Even if they committed the most heinous crime imaginable, their parents would still love them. Of course, it doesn't mean the parents would condone an evil act. It means they do not reject the child despite disapproval of the behavior. Sadly, for every child who is loved unconditionally, there's probably a child who is faced with conditional love. In this type of environment, the child receives affection and praise only after meeting expectations set by the parent. Therefore, the child feels loved only if he or she gets the A, makes the basketball team, or consistently acquiesces to the parent.

If you received a lot of unconditional positive regard throughout your life, you have examples to draw from when giving acceptance. If you didn't, the practice of giving unconditional positive regard might be more challenging. On the flip side, it might make you want to give it even more. Either way, the more you give it, the more likely you are to receive it.

The easiest way to convey your unconditional positive regard or acceptance on a date is by being nonjudgmental. Take a look at the following list of statements:

- I hate that!
- How could you do something like that?
- You're dead wrong.
- Eeewww, disssgusting.
- What?!
- No way!
- I totally disagree.
- That's not something *I* would do.

Picture yourself in the middle of a sentence as the man in your life suddenly interrupts with a phrase like one of these. Or worse, maybe he doesn't say it but looks disgusted by or disapproving of your words. If it didn't stop you dead in your tracks, it would at the very least put you on the defensive. And if it happens to be the first date, you might choose to avoid a second date.

If these statements are going to put you on the defensive, they'll make him raise his shields as well. If you want to know your date, it can't be emphasized enough that one of the single most effective ways to draw him out is to assume a nonjudgmental stance. Even if you don't say or look obvious about your disapproval, a man can smell when you're judging him.

Does this mean that you have to agree with everything he says, like a puppet with no opinion of her own? Absolutely not! Unconditional positive regard doesn't require agreement or condoning certain thoughts and behaviors; it means giving him the freedom to express who he is to you openly and honestly and creating a nonjudgmental environment of tolerance and acceptance.

Some of you may be thinking, "Wait a minute, can I be nonjudgmental and still evaluate if he's right for me?" The answer is yes. Just because you're accepting and valuing him as a fellow human being doesn't mean you have to accept him into your life and value him in a relationship with you.

BEING REAL, BEING CONGRUENT!

Essentially, congruence means that your true thoughts and feelings match your behavior. Empathy and unconditional positive regard come from a real place inside you. There will be times that, for whatever reason, you just can't muster up empathy or acceptance—that's part of being human. Maybe you're sick that day; maybe the guy grates on your one last nerve; maybe he truly expresses loathsome or cruel attitudes; maybe you plain don't like him. You'll feel much more authentic and better in the end if you're true to yourself through your behaviors (yet, of course, still being politely authentic in cases where you don't like the guy).

What happens if you do really like the guy? According to the concept of congruence, you should show it. But should you really let on that you like him? The safest bet is yes, definitely. This doesn't mean telling him on the third date that you want to have his baby. It simply means that it's okay to spontaneously let out some of those verbal and nonverbal cues that show you like someone, such as good eye contact, smiling, or simply letting him know, "I had a really good time tonight!"

The idea of congruence is counter to the hard-to-get approach. Remember, with profiling there's no need to *play* hard to get. Profiling gives you a sense of objectively and empowerment that is the antithesis of desperation. If in any way, shape, or form a guy misinterprets your congruent, authentic feelings of liking him for desperation, then it's time to profile him out of your life.

Questions and Answers

QUESTIONS ARE THE MOST OBVIOUS way to get to know a man, and they definitely have their place in conversation. The key is to find a good balance between questions and other ways to get answers from him, such as empathetic paraphrasing, discussed previously. Therapists in training are cautioned not to overly rely on questions when more subtle means are available. Nobody wants to feel like he's on the firing range or the witness stand. The man you're with will appreciate questions that are well-timed and flow naturally with the dialogue.

OPEN AND CLOSED QUESTIONS

There are two kinds of questions: open and closed. Open questions are general, broad-based questions to which the answer can't be yes or no. The following are examples of open questions:

- Can you tell me what it was like growing up in the city?
- What do you think about the people running for president?
- So what does a day in the life of an investment banker look like?
- As a doctor, how do you deal with illness on a day-to-day basis? How does it make you feel?

As you can see, these questions leave someone with a lot of wiggle room to answer. Some men are more comfortable than others with open questions, because answering an open question requires him to expose his beliefs, values, ideas, and emotions to you. One way to draw him out is to give thoughtful and detailed responses to his open questions so that you serve as an example to him.

In contrast to open questions, closed questions tend to be focused and home in on specific areas. They allow a man to give a one- or two-word response. The following are examples of closed questions:

- Is your boss easy to get along with?
- Who did you vote for in the last election?
- How many brothers and sisters do you have?
- What was your degree in?

Clearly, these are fact-finding types of questions. Quiet or shy men are probably more apt to be at home with these kinds of questions;

however, although you don't want to push, you also don't want to let the guy off the hook with a bunch of boring yes and no answers. Striking a balance between both open and closed questions is important so that you get a good mix of short and long responses and a natural flow of conversation.

FOLLOW-UP QUESTIONS

If he gets to a topic that you want to know more about, follow-up questions are always an option. For example, if all he gives you is his job title, you can follow up by asking what kinds of things his job entails.

Again, don't forget to explore the more subtle ways of squeezing juice from this orange. For example, when you are intrigued by something he is saying and want to follow up, give him positive reinforcement. A nonverbal smile or nod, as well as a verbal "uh-huh," "hmmm," or "That's really interesting!" can work wonders.

"TELL ME WHAT I WANT TO HEAR"

It's easy to fall into the trap of hoping that this man is "the one" and wishing for shared commonalities that don't exist. Unfortunately, doing this might give men carte blanche to misrepresent themselves or lie, because they can sense when a woman prefers hoping and wishing to reality and truth. However, no matter how hard we try to avoid it, reality is always around the corner waiting for a run-in with our hopes. It's much better to be prepared for the collision.

One major way that women slip into the tell-me-what-I-want-to-hear mode is by asking leading questions that have opinions and biases built into them. Essentially, leading questions are set up for one right answer. Take a look at the following:

LEADING QUESTION	BIAS-FREE QUESTION
Don't you think Jon Bon Jovi was one of the best singers ever?	Who are some of your favorite singers?
You don't seem like the type who is a sports addict. I mean you aren't, are you?	Are you into sports?
Every time I pick up a paper or turn on the TV, I hear about this stupid trial. I'm sooo sick of hearing about it. You must be sick of it too?	What do you think about the trial?

It's not that you don't want to share your own opinions with him; it's just that you want to create an environment in which he feels free to share as well. More bias-free questions help you to find out about the real him as opposed to the modified man.

OURS IS NOT TO QUESTION WHY

Most therapists are repeatedly reminded not to ask questions beginning with "Why?" because that tends to put people on the defensive. When you ask "Why?" you want to know the *reason* for someone's thoughts, feelings, or actions. In everyday language, it has come to have quite a demanding, critical tone.

Remember the last time someone said to you, "Why did you do *that*?" The implication is "Why'd ya do that, stupid?" Chances are, you didn't care to share openly and honestly with the person at that moment. The last thing any of us wants is to drive a man into a self-protective mode when we're trying to get the truth out of him. The answers to "Why" questions tend to get laced with spite, anger, and mistrust.

Try the "Why" substitutes below the next time you're with a man and see how they work. You're likely to be pleasantly surprised.

WHY?	WHY . . . NOT!
Why did you do that?	Tell me more about that.
Why do you feel this way?	What made you feel that way?
Why did you go out with her?	So you two dated? or How did you and she get involved?
Why did you decide to move?	How did the move come about?

AVOIDING AN INQUISITION

While women are often comfortable sitting face-to-face, one-on-one for a heart-to-heart, men usually are not. If you bring up a deep question, a thought that's been on your mind, or pose the famous question, "Can we talk?" you're liable to trigger an emotional shutdown. He may have a confused look or a blank stare and engage in a lot of stuttering. Some men may behave as if they're in captivity, ready to be interrogated by the enemy. Under these conditions, all the "enemy" is going to get out of this guy is the emotional equivalent to name, rank, and serial number.

Rather than shining an inquisitor's light in your guy's eyes every time you have a question, try this instead: Talk to him while he's doing a less-than-major task. If the task is something of major importance to him, it won't work. The requirement is that he's doing something physical that doesn't take a lot of mental effort. In other words, a small distraction from "the talk." Talking while walking, cooking, or fixing something minor are all good scenarios. You can tailor the situation to fit the guy.

By combining the mental and the physical, you create an atmosphere in which he is more likely to be comfortable. Typically, men have been socialized to relate to each other while they engage in activities. It's not unusual for women to get together and talk, but it is for men. Playing games from golf to poker to watching a sport on TV are often the centerpiece of get-togethers for men. So if you want him to be relaxed and less on guard before you dig into the conversation, remember both talking and doing.

Active Listening

ACTIVELY LISTENING TO A MAN means that you do more than simply hear what he's saying; you are also processing the meaning of the words and gestures that he is communicating to you. Because it's active and not passive, listening like this requires an exchange of energy and can actually be physically tiring. The rewards of active listening, however, are great. Think about the warm feelings you've had inside when a man really tries to hear what you're saying. Now think about the cold feelings you've had inside when a man lets your words drop dead at his feet. If you're interested in a man, it's important to leave him with those awesome, warm feelings.

Most of you may be thinking, "I'm a pretty good listener already." And it's probably true. However, as you take a closer look, you might single out some areas for improvement. Look over the following list and put check marks by the listening faux pas that you have committed during conversations with a man you are (or were) interested in.

Active Listening Checklist

___ Interrupting his stream of thought with your own stream

___ Breaking silences or pauses in the conversation too quickly (he may be reflecting during these gaps)

___ Letting your eyes wander or glaze over a lot while he is talking to you

___ Not asking for clarification when you don't quite get what he has said

___ Misunderstanding the intent of his words

___ Thinking about what you're going to say next while he's talking

___ Jumping in quickly with, "Oh, that's something, but it doesn't even come close to what happened to me" or "That reminds me, did I tell you what happened to me the other day?"

___ Half listening to what he is saying and half attending to something else

___ Carelessly intruding with quick-fix advice

___ Listening without really *listening*! This means that you're taking in his words without mentally processing them.

If you notice several check marks, don't feel guilty; simply practice some of the following listening techniques on your next date.

FOCUSING ON YOUR DATE: BODY AND MIND

In a world of multitasking, it's so easy not to pay attention to what's important. A lot of meaningful interactions can slip by and not get noticed. The following suggestions will help you focus, body and mind, so that you will really notice your date. You'll find that by using these techniques, he will also really notice you!

Listening Hear *and Now*

So often, individuals live out of the moment. As words are being spoken to them, their thoughts may race from past to future and back to past again. They aren't able to connect with what is being said at present, and this lack of connection is felt by the listener. It's palpable when someone is not in the *"hear* and now."

As part of before-the-date training to get that focus back, try the "bubble technique." In conversations with family and friends, start to pay attention to when stray thoughts enter your mind while they are talking. Oops, a thing from your to-do list just popped in, didn't it? And a worry about work? The nuances and subtleties of what the person said may escape you while you are distracted.

It's not easy to clear out the clutter of thoughts you've become accustomed to holding on to, because often, the more you try to stop thoughts from coming into your head, the more intrusive they become. To help with this, in the beginning, imagine each stray thought as a bubble that just floats by and then pops, enabling you to clear your head and regain focus in the present.

As you develop your ability to concentrate more fully, you'll be floored by the amount of detailed information you get, as well as a more in-depth understanding of the object of focus. The great thing is that by being present for your date in this way, you add texture and richness to the entire dating experience. The man you're with will surely sense this.

Listening with Your Body

"As the body goes, so goes the mind."[3] Such is the core of yoga philosophy. If you create comfortable body movement and rhythm for yourself on a date, you create a more comfortable date for both you and him.

A body position that says you're open and ready to listen will coax him into talking. Leaning into him, good eye contact, and a facial expression that says, "Tell me more," are important. Also, try to achieve a settled-in feel where you're sitting. Do you look relaxed and comfy, or do you look like you're ready to leap out of your seat at any moment? Fidgeting can be a real distraction.

Another essential posturing technique is mirroring, in which you subtly reflect his body language in your body language. Think of it as absorbing his movement and giving it back to him. For example, say he is telling a story with anxious eyes, a clenched jaw, and ridged torso. You'll get into it more if you mirror his posture with whatever movement feels natural to you. Additionally, listening to his edge-of-the-seat story with something like wide eyes and clenched fists is going to show you are interested and make him want to continue much more than if you just sit there.

You may have noticed, when talking about posture, that words like "rhythm," "body," "movement," and "positions" are used. It can all be very sensual, not unlike sharing a dance with someone. Communicating well with your body adds another dimension to a conversation that can make a date with you extraordinary. Everyone speaks with body language. The trick is to be more aware of its power to unleash dialogue and to allow a greater flow of both verbal and nonverbal communication between two people.

Shhhhh . . . Silence Doesn't Have to Be Awkward

Oh, how women fear the wince-inducing, awkward silence on a date! If the pause is clumsy and self-conscious enough, it may eat through our gut. And because there are no nonverbal cues on the phone, silences during a call can seem even more deadly.

Because these awkward pauses are dreaded, sometimes women overcompensate. Many rush to fill a gap in the conversation with fast chatter, a nervous giggle, or a quick change of topic. The problem is that the awkwardness of continuously keeping the conversation on fast-forward can be just as bad as a lull-filled tête-à-tête.

A fun and informative activity to try is tape recording yourself during a conversation with a friend (to avoid any juicy scandals or legal issues, please inform the friend that he or she is being taped). As you play back the conversation, notice the number and length of pauses. Are there places where you jumped in too quickly? Are there times where you could have allowed for a pause? Chances are, the more comfortable you feel with the person, the more silences you allowed.

Researchers found that interviewers who create a comfortable environment and elicit a lot of talk allow pauses of at least four or five seconds many times during a conversation.[4] Often when people listen to their own taped conversations, they feel there were too few pauses rather than too many. What do you think about your own tape?

It's not usually thought of this way, but encouraging silence actually encourages deeper talk. Nobody knows this better than therapists. Allowing a silent moment now and then helps people to collect their thoughts, focus on the meaning of their words, and perhaps more accurately express what they are trying to say.

Because your aim is to listen and learn about your date, some well-timed silences help by cajoling more of his personality out. Therapists are aware that by invading pauses too quickly, they can lead the conversation away from what their client is thinking about. When you're trying to get to know a man, it's important to let him take the lead sometimes in order to see where he is going. He may go in a direction you would never have guessed—for good or for bad.

None of this is to say that you should just sit there, stare at the guy, and wait for him to say something next. Just like with body language, practicing silence is about rhythm. As you develop more awareness of it, you will get a sense for what constitutes an awkward silence versus a contemplative pause.

The goal here is to create a comfortable environment through the use of well-timed silence. As with the practice of being present in the moment and the practice of posture, the practice of silence creates a secure space for talk. Although the man you're with may not be able to put his finger on it, he will wonder what it is about you that makes talking come so naturally.

LISTENING FOR SUBTEXT

Men don't always say what they mean, which is why it's important to actively listen to their words, as well as to the reality behind them. There are often subtle undercurrents to polite statements, subconscious meanings behind neutral comments, and various connotations to a given statement. Take a look at the following:

HE SAYS . . .	HE MEANS . . .
It's challenging.	It's a pain in the ass!
That's psychobabble.	Don't analyze me.
You got a haircut.	I hate your haircut.
That's an interesting dress.	I don't like that dress.
It's not you, it's me.	It's you.
I need space.	I want to break up.
I'm really focused on my career.	I don't want to commit.
That restaurant is too fancy.	I'm cheap when it comes to you.

Okay, the last one may seem a little callous, but it does happen.

To an extent, this kind of undercurrent or subtext is a normal part of conversation. We all do it consciously to be polite, as well as subconsciously. The trouble is when the whole conversation becomes subtext. If the guy you're with is always hinting at things and never quite saying what he means, that's poor communication and possibly indicative of deeper issues. No one can be expected to actively listen to subtext 24/7. In these cases, it's important to encourage your date/boyfriend to say what he means.

Besides making yourself crazy with a guy who is oversubtexted, you also don't want to overinterpret dialogue. How many of us have obsessed for days over four or five words a guy has said to us? "Does he mean this?" "Could it be that?" Analyzing his words to death can take the spontaneity and fun out of things, plus make you paranoid. If a statement of his is on your mind so much, it's probably a good idea to discuss it further with him to try to discern his true meaning and either confirm or alleviate your worries. It's more than likely that he'll sense your suspiciousness anyway.

LISTENING BEYOND CONTENT

Besides devoting yourself to content, which is the real raw meat of the conversation, it's important to attend to the goings-on and inner workings of the conversation. This includes paying attention to your surroundings, the contours of the conversation, and other tactics and maneuvers both on your part and his. The following are some questions to think about when you're talking with him:

TIMING. Is he squirming in his seat because you've been sitting and talking in one place too long? Is the phone conversation dragging on to the point that your ear hurts?

SELF-MONITORING. Are your questions making him uncomfortable? Are they too personal too soon? Are many of your statements judgmental?

MAN MONITORING. Is he being attentive to you? Do his questions, statements, and gestures indicate he is interested in you? Is he a good active listener?

ATMOSPHERE. If you set conversation as the goal of your being together, is the atmosphere conducive to talk? Are you trying to talk in a loud club where you probably should be dancing instead? Are you bothering him with too much conversation at a sporting event? Is the setting too public? Too intimate?

TONE. Is this turning into an aggressive exchange? Is it becoming a therapy session? (We want to borrow some techniques from therapists, not turn a date into actual therapy.) Are you sounding like a supervisor, professor, lawyer? Is he? Is it turning into a grilling session? Is it boring? If so, how could you add spark to the chat?

A Climate of Comfort

THE TECHNIQUES DISCUSSED in this chapter combine to create a climate of comfort for you and the man you're interested in. A climate of comfort is a zone of freedom, which includes empathic understanding and acceptance. It's a place where two people can be themselves and share parts of themselves with one another. Helping to create this kind of environment is something special, and that specialness will be felt.

More often than not, as you work to create a climate of comfort with a man, chances are he will intuit the atmosphere you are creating and add to it. When people sense something special, they usually want to be a part of it, not stand outside of it.

Of course, as we all know, developing a climate of comfort does not mean that you automatically establish a love connection. The fact is that you are more than likely to establish a connection by getting to know each other in this way. Where connections may lead is anybody's guess—it could be to friendship, companionship, or something wonderfully romantic.

Sketch His Profile

IN MANY WAYS, finding what you want requires first knowing what you want. Before you can connect with a date, you need to sketch out a profile of the type of man you're looking for. Then you can compare and contrast this profile with the men you meet. You're e-*value*-ating your date to determine if he's right for you. Do you value him as a partner? Do you value being in a relationship with him? You're making the judgment as to whether you and this man can develop a worthwhile romantic connection.

The Profile

IN ORDER TO SKETCH your unique guy profile, you need to spend some time thinking about what you want, tweaking your subconscious into giving up some information, as well as letting your conscious mind run free. See what kind of responses the following questions elicit from you:

- What qualities in men make you smile?
- What bad boyfriend habits have you overlooked in the past?
- What behaviors signal strength of character?
- In what ways do men show depth of feeling?
- What does compassion mean to you?
- Define fun.
- What makes a man unattractive?
- What do you immediately respond to in men?
- Have you ever surprised yourself by liking something about a guy that you didn't know you liked?

Now that you've gone over these questions, your mind should be more limber and your thoughts flowing freely. It's time to begin writing down characteristics that will comprise your delicious man profile. What are fifteen qualities that you would like your man to have?

1. _____

2. _____

3. _____

4. _____

5. _____

6. _____

7. _____

8. _____

9. _____

10. _____

11. _____

12. _____

13. _____

14. _____

15. _____

    The next and last step in sketching his profile is to condense your fifteen characteristics into one or two descriptive sentences. Condensing will help to crystallize your thoughts and give you a focus in terms of the guy you're looking for. Here's an example:

The man I want is <u>bright, empathic, good-looking, and fun. He shares many of my interests, including being outdoors and loving animals, but most important of all is his unshakable love for me!</u>

_____

    Now you try.

The man I want is _____

_____

_____

_____

_____

_____

There it is—the knowledge of what you want in one or two sentences. Congratulations! It's no small feat.

A Positive Vision

AFTER COMPLETING THE PROFILE, some of you are going to feel wonderful because you find that the profile of the man in your life, at least to some degree, matches the profile you're looking for. You've just confirmed that the man you're dating, seeing exclusively, or living with may potentially be the right fit for you. It's scary, but it's also a beautiful feeling to know that this relationship is looking pretty good!

Others may be saying, "Wait a minute! I haven't come across this guy, this guy isn't in my life now, and this guy may never be in my life." Before you start sinking into a sea of depression, hold on because here comes the life preserver.

The life preserver presents itself in the form of a positive vision of the future. One of the main things successful people have in common is an optimistic image of what lies ahead. They imagine their life story unfolding as they want it to be, even under the most dire circumstances.

The renowned psychologist Viktor Frankl used his positive vision of the future to cope with and ultimately survive the brutality of a concentration camp. To escape the horror of the present, he imagined himself in the future giving lectures about the psychology of survival and the truths he learned during the time of his imprisonment. In the end, his positive mental pictures turned into positive realities. His psychological theories have inspired countless people.[1]

There probably isn't a more different character from Viktor Frankl than Donald Trump, real estate mogul, reality TV guru, and over-the-top egoist. Yet juxtaposing these two men, each successful in his own way, proves a point. Creating the future they wanted was in a large part about envisioning what they wanted and going after it. Trump often speaks about the importance of energy, optimism, and having vision.

What Frankl accomplished in personal survival and in psychology, and Trump in business, you need to apply to your relationship. It's all-important to have faith in the future—faith that someone resembling the profile you just created is out there for you. Even when things look the worst and you've just come back from a date with your millionth loser, it's still important to see that guy 1,000,001 may have some potential.

But it's not enough to daydream about the million-and-one man. Meeting him, knowing him, and relating to him all require action. It's necessary to set achievable goals and to take steps to get there. Profiling is an achievable process and an active process. With profiling, you take steps to fulfill your vision. You get to know different personalities, make connections with new people, and discover what's right for you and your future.

Life might not hand us exactly whom you want, or exactly when you want, but life does present us with countless opportunities, possibilities, surprises, and miniadventures. Women who learn to take advantage of what life gives us, rather than what it doesn't, tend to be happier and more fulfilled.

The Airport Security Model of Finding Men

HAVE YOU NOTICED how airports profile for potential hijackers? Seemingly at random, you may have received a sticker during check-in indicating that your baggage would be singled out for extra security scrutiny, or perhaps at a security checkpoint you appeared to be randomly picked to undergo additional security procedures.

But as we hear in the media, some very specific people and/or behavior may be profiled for. Airport security may be looking for precise characteristics that could be indicative of danger. An agitated person with a one-way ticket paid for in cash is a hypothetical example of a profile type.

The parallel here with dating men is that you want to do random checks as well as profile for specific characteristics.

Comparing your profile of what you want to the men you meet or are currently dating is profiling for specific characteristics. It's great to have an idea of what you want in a man. The problem is that after completing your profile, you might experience the temptation to laminate it and carry it in your wallet. This is the trap of sticking rigidly to the profile you've created.

In order to stay out of that trap, you need to do some random profiling as well, which simply means that you want to give men that may not seem to be your type a try. In this way, you allow the universe to send you a surprise. Who knows? Maybe it turns out you like some quality or characteristic that you never knew you liked. Or maybe the combination of qualities in a man equals more than the sum of his parts. Don't be afraid to deviate from what you think is right for you.

You don't want to set your sights so myopically on one specific type of man that you miss the awesome guy standing right in front of you. Building rigid profiles can not only make you miss a good guy, but it can also take a toll on relationships. Have you ever tried to cram a guy into your mold when it clearly did not fit him?

Think of the profile you developed as a sketch in progress. Sketches can be added to and taken away from. Particularly, as you read through *Profiling Your Date*, you'll find that tweaks and changes to the profile you've created are par for the course. This is good. Profiles often morph into something more beautiful than what you started out with.

Sexual Attraction, Chemistry, and Phero-*moans*

IT IS FRUSTRATING when a guy who looks good on paper—pleasant personality, stable job, and nice friends—just doesn't do it for you. After going out with him, you're left feeling empty and disappointed. Still, you try again and try forcing yourself to like him because you believe you *should* like him.

It's not that anything's really wrong with him; it's that something is missing, and you believe that maybe if you try hard enough you'll be able to find that missing thing. Yet no matter what you do (guzzle wine before you have to kiss him) or how hard you try (one mediocre date turns into six), it's just not there with this guy.

The thing that you're probably missing with him is chemistry. But what exactly is chemistry? Put simply, it's a spark of attraction between two people. Chemistry is that magnetic tug of desire—the stuff that pulls you toward someone, often without you even knowing why. Of course, a big part of the pull is sexual, but that's not the entirety of it. Chemistry is all-encompassing.

Chemistry is also something for which you're always subconsciously profiling. The spark for another person happens below the surface, just under your level of awareness, and perhaps at a biological, animal level.

Animal Instincts

PHEROMONES ARE CHEMICALS emitted by animals that cause physiological or endocrine changes in the receiving animal. Research into human pheromones is still relatively incomplete, yet some studies show pheromones can affect human relationships.

MALE PHEROMONES: HEATING US UP OR COOLING US DOWN?

In one recent study, researchers put male underarm "secretions," thought to contain pheromones under women's noses.[1] It was found that these pheromones had the power to alter the length and timing of menstruation due to their effect on women's luteinizing hormone (LH) levels. Moreover, upon exposure to the male pheromones, women actually felt more relaxed and less tense. We all know that in both good ways and bad, men can bring us to the boiling point. It's nice to have some scientific backing that, yeah, they can make us feel cool, calm, and collected as well.

ANOTHER SWEATY STUDY

One of the major pieces of evidence that experts cite regarding pheromone-type research is the Swiss sweaty T-shirt study.[2] In the study, forty-nine male university students were asked to wear cotton T-shirts for two days without using any soap, deodorants, and so on. Afterward, forty-nine female university students were asked to smell six shirts each and rate them in terms of sexiness.

Researchers were looking to see if the women sniffed out immunity genes, called the major histocompatibility complex (MHC), which are very closely linked to pheromone-generating genes. The different genes in the MHC are what give us immunity to disease. They are also what could cause us to reject an organ transplant if there is no MHC compatibility between the donor and the recipient.

Each woman whiffed three T-shirts from men who had dissimilar MHCs from her own and three that were similar. The sexier the women ranked the T-shirts, the more dissimilar the men's MHCs were from their own. In other words, the women were able to detect the MHC and preferred men with different immunity genes from themselves.

It's speculated that one reason women may naturally select men with dissimilar immunity genes is that it acts as sort of an incest preventative. Fathers, brothers, cousins, and other kin are more likely to be MHC-similar with a woman. Genetically, inbreeding is considered unhealthy for a species; so theoretically, the MHC factor forces a woman to broaden her horizons and to choose a genetically dissimilar mate. This mixing of different genes leads to more robust offspring, and in this case perhaps more comprehensive immune defenses.

CAN PRESCRIPTION MEDS THROW YOU OFF THE SCENT?

For women taking birth control pills, the results of the sweaty T-shirt study were reversed. Women on the pill preferred T-shirts from the MHC-similar men.

This suggests that birth control pills could be affecting our choices in men and potentially not in an optimum way. Could it be that birth control pills are screwing up sensors we didn't even know we had? Additional research is being done in this area so that we can have more definitive answers.

One thing's for sure: It's amazing to realize that birth control pills and other medications we're taking could play a role in mate selection beyond our awareness. For example, think about the adverse sexual side effects that the pill can have, as well as popular SSRI (selective serotonin reuptake inhibitor) antidepressants such as Prozac. Both types of pills are known to decrease libido in some women.[3]

This means that many of us are dating without our normal sex drive, which has serious implications for picking a partner. What if a woman chooses someone with a low sex drive to match hers but then goes off medication only to find out her libido is in overdrive? What if a couple that is frustrated, because his sexual appetite is huge and hers is portion-controlled, finds it is all due to medication?

Women who began taking these types of prescriptions at a young age may have no understanding of their nonchemically altered sexual drives. Obviously, this is not to say that women should stop taking their medications; they are prescribed for a reason. However, it is a good idea to talk with physicians about these issues so that you can make informed choices. Simply being aware of medications' possible effects on chemistry and relationships goes a long way.

Secret Agents of Love

SO WHAT OTHER UNDERCOVER agents are involved in the chemistry of love? Researchers are finding that a complex web of neurotransmitters and hormones have a big influence on our falling and staying in love. Phenylethylamine (PEA) and oxytocin are just two among an array of interacting agents that shape the way we love.[4]

PHENYLETHYLAMINE

Phenylethylamine is the happy juice that our brains release when we have new love feelings for someone. It's an endorphin that acts like speed, causing our heart rates and blood pressure to increase, as well as giving us that high-on-love sensation.

Fortunately, if you've been experiencing a shortage of new loves lately, there's always chocolate. And what makes chocolate so special? Leave it to scientists to uncover part of chocolate's mysterious allure. They've found that cocoa contains PEA.

The thing about the PEA high, with love and with chocolate, is that it's relatively temporary. Really, if you think about it, who could sustain that euphoric type of love constantly? You and your lover would spontaneously combust. Many new couples, fogged in by the PEA cloud, have sex until they drop. Who could maintain that pace forever?

Besides, you wouldn't want your common sense clouded by PEA forever. This love high may cause you to overlook a lot of big red flags waving in the wind. You might also overlook significant compatibility issues, such as value differences and divergent life goals. PEA may cause confusion between lasting love and simple lust.

Some might argue that ignorance is bliss and wish they could get lost permanently in the bloom of love. At first glance, this might seem like a fun option. There are men and women who get so caught in the fix that they seek out new love as if it were heroin. They're addicted to losing themselves in passionate love. However, to get lost in love means to lose oneself, and that's never a good option.

As with many things, moderation seems to be the best answer. Go ahead and enjoy your new, passionate love, just don't get entirely blinded.

Also ask yourself key questions to determine your pattern of loving as well as your partner's. Do you move from fresh catch to fresh catch? Do you feel addicted to the newness of love? Does he have a history of bolting after the PEA levels drop? Do you tend to idealize the new men in your life? Does he idealize new girlfriends?

OXYTOCIN

After about six months, or maybe a year, or two, or three, PEA stops working its insane magic. What happens then? Happily, oxytocin, the "cuddle hormone," is there to cushion the fall. Oxytocin is responsible for enduring pair-bonding in animals. It helps foster attachments between romantic partners, as well as between parents and children and other loved ones.

You know that comfortable and content feeling when you're touched, held, or hugged by someone you love. To a large degree, oxytocin deserves the credit. Researchers are also looking at the role of oxytocin in our attachment to a loved one's features.[5] They theorize that when we gaze at a loved one or someone who looks similar to a loved one, oxytocin gets triggered, giving us a warm, fuzzy feeling. In this way, it helps us to bond with our loved ones, as well as to form prototypes of whom we find attractive. Oxytocin may be partially to blame when we're attracted to the same types again and again.

As an added point of interest, this fabulous hormone helps get the smooth muscle contracting in the uterus, hopefully contributing to a great orgasm during sex! With oxytocin in tow, there's really no need to mourn the loss of PEA with too much vigor.

Pheromones, PEA, and oxytocin are just a few of the covert concoctions our bodies produce to stimulate interest (or in some cases, lack of interest) in mating. Others include dopamine, estrogen, and testosterone. The point here is to develop an awareness of how strong a role the biology inside of us plays when we're profiling. Awareness can help you use that information to your advantage!

Attraction and Beauty Paradox

BEAUTY, BOTH INSIDE AND OUTSIDE, is a major player in the chemistry component. Beautiful men put smiles on our faces and add bright spots to our days. Inner and outer beauty may not be the whole of chemistry, but chemistry certainly does seem dependent on it. Take a minute to ponder these two statements about beauty.

Beauty is in the eye of the beholder.
There are universal standards of beauty.

These statements contradict each other, yet both seem true. Each of us has his or her own quirks about whom we consider to be beautiful; hence, "Beauty is in the eye of the beholder." Yet a majority of us could probably agree on the physical attractiveness of certain men, such as George Clooney, Jude Law, Denzel Washington, and Antonio Banderas; hence, "There are universal standards of beauty."

UNIQUE BEAUTY

First, let's explore where your unique vision of beauty comes from. Without getting too psychoanalytical, your past could be playing a big part regarding whom you find attractive in personality and in looks. For example, a woman's attraction to men with big, brown, puppy dog eyes might stem from the love of her father's warm, kind eyes. Or perhaps she feels drawn to men who are energetic and athletic because a lot of the men in her family were that way.

More dangerously, women can become attracted to traits that they are accustomed to yet make for unhealthy relationships. For example, a woman who constantly had to vie for her father's attention might seek out emotionally unavailable men. Or a woman who has been physically abused may now feel chemistry with men who strike her.

Past emotional, sexual, or physical abuse can impact a woman's attraction for a man with such a pervasive force that it's too much for one person to have to sort through herself. Enlisting the help of a psychotherapist makes the process of delving into and sorting out the past more systematic, less isolated, and usually very productive.

From a therapist's perspective, it's important to bring to the surface the knowledge of the type of men who do attract you, do not attract you, and why. You may not be able to figure why completely; however, you can achieve a bit more insight over a period of time.

At least partially figuring out what pulls you toward certain men will put your attraction in context. If you're dating someone, placing the source of your attraction could actually make you more attracted to him or, in some cases, less attracted to him. There are a lot of dysfunctional relationships in which this kind of chemical attraction acts as a bad glue bond. Figuring out why the glue is so sticky can help you to break free.

To gain some insight into what attracts you, take a look at the following questions:

- Who were your favorite movie, TV, and literary characters as a child? What do they have in common?
- Was there a male family member who was often kind to you as a child? What did he look like? What were his personality characteristics?
- Was there a male family member who was often cruel to you as a child? What did he look like? What were his personality characteristics?

- Who are some of your favorite movie stars now? How are they alike?
- What kinds of looks are most familiar and comfortable to you? Which are you unaccustomed to?
- What is your definition of sexy?
- What is "masculine" to you?
- Who was your first crush?
- What personality characteristics are beautiful to you?
- In your fantasies, what does the man usually look like? How have your fantasies changed over the years?

Pick the career on this list that attracts you the most:

artist	entrepreneur	policeman
stockbroker	builder	landscaper
engineer	doctor	professor

THE UNIVERSALS OF BEAUTY

There seem to be some physical attributes that we as a species find attractive. You may actually be reacting to some of these attributes at a gut level without being particularly cognizant of them. The following are some universal attributes of fabulous faces:[6]

STRAIGHT PROFILE. The jaw is aligned with the forehead so that the chin doesn't jut way inward or way outward.

SYMMETRY. One side of the face is about the same as the other side. Crooked teeth fall under the category of asymmetrical.

YOUTH. There is perceived beauty in a youthful face more often than in an aged one.

AVERAGENESS. In many nineteenth-century novels, the heroes and heroines often were described as having "regular features." This regularity, or "averageness," is often rated as attractive.

GENDER CONSISTENCY. Men tend to have larger jaws and noses yet smaller eyes and cheekbones than women. Females are inclined to be attracted to male faces that follow these standards of "maleness."

FAMILIARITY. The more familiar the face, the more attractive it becomes—even when the face is not consciously recognized as familiar.

For every example of a universally beautiful face, we all could come up with counterexamples. Often beauty and sexuality can be found in expressive, exotic, or eccentric features.

Due to complications at birth, Sylvester Stallone has one eye lower than the other and a very asymmetrical face. It hasn't stopped his movie career or sex symbol status. David Letterman doesn't have a youthful face, but he sure does have a lot of female guests hanging on him. What about James Gandolfini, aka Tony Soprano? Not an average face, yet a highly charismatic, expressive one. Then there's Jack Nicholson's face. . . .

The idea is that so many variables can factor into a fabulous face, including the uniqueness of the face itself, the man behind the face, and the perceiver of the face, which in this case is you.

Going back full circle to hormones, your menstrual cycle can also affect which men's faces you find attractive.[7] One study found that during their most fertile time of the month, women preferred more masculine-looking male faces (for example, larger jaws). Whereas during their least fertile time, women preferred more feminine-looking male faces.

This study is just one example of how our attraction for a man can vary over time. Chemistry can be fickle and fleeting. What does this mean for profiling your date? It means that in some instances you might want to give a guy you're not initially highly attracted to another chance. Maybe he'll strike you more positively at another time, in another place, or at a different phase of your menstrual cycle!

Do Opposites Attract?

THE IDEA OF OPPOSITES attracting gets a lot of verbal play in conversations about dating. And there is some truth in it. It can be nice to find someone with a quality we lack ourselves. If you're shy, maybe an extroverted guy can coax you out of your shell. Or maybe a laid-back guy can add a little calm to an overly ordered existence.

But, and this is a big *but*, most of the time we are seeking someone similar to ourselves. In fact, the drive toward commonality is so powerful that we may not even consciously realize the strength of the pull. Maybe it's because we're comfortable with what's familiar. Or maybe we feel that the best chance of being understood is with a man like ourselves. Whatever the reason, it's important to be aware of our own attraction to a mirror of ourselves!

One study in particular found that women preferred partners who were similar with regard to traits such as boldness, activeness, warmth, kindness, responsibility, intelligence, perceptiveness, and creativity.[8] If the women were low in these traits, they wanted someone low too. If they were high in the traits, they wanted someone high.

Now is a good time to examine some of your own traits, characteristics, and beliefs. Then think of past/present boyfriends and how they differed from you or were similar regarding the following:

- socioeconomic status
- politics
- religion
- cultural/racial/ethnic background
- education
- IQ
- looks
- hobbies/interests

Chemistry: When to Give It Up, When to Turn It Up?

ALTHOUGH CHEMISTRY HAS to do with sexual attraction, there is so much more to it. A lot goes on at a physiological level, including hormones and pheromones. There is also a wealth of psychological variables interacting with the physiological that affect whom we are drawn to and whom we find inwardly and outwardly beautiful.

Yet it's still not possible to pinpoint chemistry absolutely and definitively. There are several secret ingredients churning together in a rather mysterious way. This is not necessarily bad! The unexplained element in chemistry accounts for much of its strength.

PROFILING FOR CHEMISTRY

Sometimes chemistry is the easiest thing to profile for. You meet a guy, and BAM! you're struck seemingly beyond conscious control. At other times, chemistry may creep up on you slowly but surely.

Many married couples say that the chemistry was more the tortoise than the hare. One study showed that women who accept a second or third date with men they're not so chemically attracted to in the beginning often end up happily married to them.[9]

This is a fine line. There comes a point in a relationship where if it hasn't happened, it's not going to. The specific timing of this point is personal and depends on the situation. Four to six dates feels like a lot if you're not finding yourself drawn to this person. However, some people have been known to give it four to six months or even four to six years! Lisa, a twenty-eight-year-old stockbroker, calls it "beating a relationship to death," but she says she needs to or else she'll regret her decision about breaking up. There are also women who choose men with whom they have no chemistry because of other advantages the relationship provides. Linda, a fifty-year-old teacher, describes her twenty-year marriage as always lacking that special thing, yet she and her husband are companions who respect one another and created two beautiful children together. Would you rather be in a stable relationship without chemistry, or take the risk of waiting for a relationship with chemistry?

Most of us would probably agree that you can't create chemistry out of thin air. However, it's not something that's completely out of our control, either. Profiling harnesses that control. For example, if you profile your date as having good chemistry and bad behavior, you need to work on snuffing out the spark. On the other hand, if your profiling antennae sense a good guy with spark potential, try nurturing that chemistry.

BUILDING AND SMASHING ASSOCIATIONS

The idea is to turn it up with Healthy Relationship Guy and give it up with Dysfunctional Guy. The question then becomes, How? Reading through this chapter, you've probably noticed that a lot of chemistry is created through largely unconscious associations that women need to become consciously aware of through a self-reflective process that may include activities such as journaling, developing insights into the past, or therapy.

For instance, a woman who had sensuous sex with a flaky writer in college has now become consciously aware that she makes the association between flaky writers and great sex. Every time she meets a flaky writer she gets a physiological rush plus all these sexy images racing through her mind, which reinforce the association even more. Now this woman wants to get married, but the only men she has chemistry with are flaky writer types. She has effectively limited her pool of marriageable men to zero.

Not to worry! She built the association, now she can smash it! Smashing associations requires that you connect something negative with the positive. Here are a few things to try.

Smashing Bad Boy Associations

- Paste his picture next to a list of terrible things he has done to you. Hang it on the wall at eye level, so you get the full impact every time you enter the room.
- Conjure an image of something vile and disgusting— maggots, vomit, festering wounds, etc. Then, every time you think of him or feel attracted to him, call upon that image. Do it over and over for it to be effective.
- Every time you find yourself daydreaming about him, literally talk to yourself out loud about all his bad qualities.
- If you profile a lot of red flags, hold off sleeping with him, because that's likely to get you hooked on him.
- As much as possible, keep yourself from dwelling on all the chemistry with him. It reinforces the association. Distract yourself with your own creative pursuits.

- Put a rubber band around your wrist. Every time you have a sexy thought about him, snap it!
- Smash the old bad associations by creating good new ones with someone else.

By building good chemical associations, you add positives on top of positives. Here are a few suggestions to help you fan the flames. Can you think of other innovative ideas?

Building Good Guy Connections

- Increase the fun factor! Invite him to events that you really enjoy, so the fun gets connected with the guy.
- Ride a roller coaster or eat spicy food together. Maybe you'll associate the adrenaline rush with him.
- Create an air of romance around him by creating romantic situations. Put on a sexy CD. Light candles. Watch a great love story.
- Make a list of very specific things you find attractive about him—his strong hands, the happy expression on his face when he sees you, the way he makes you laugh, and so on. Read it frequently.

If the start of something is there, these association builders should make a difference. If the harder you try, the more you are re-pelled and revolted, blow out the candles, turn off the CD, and call it a night. There are too many men out there to torture yourself with sour chemistry!

When You and He Click, but the Sex Doesn't

Here's a tough situation: You're absolutely, ravenously attracted to the man you're seeing; you've profiled him as someone with real potential; and after an exciting buildup of sexual tension over the course of time, you decide to sleep with him. After all that anticipation, all those exuberant expectations, all the erotic buildup, the sex falls flat!

It's not that you didn't enjoy being with him or weren't attracted to him. It's just that your orgasm, which has made an appearance in other relationships (and perhaps alone), seems to have disappeared. And it's the same thing the next time you're with him, and the next . . . fulfillment nowhere to be found.

Except for in the movies (new sexual encounters in film are always portrayed with no shortage of panting and gasping on the woman's part), this scenario is quite common and no cause for alarm.

The female anatomy is somewhat complex in that women usually need a little more maneuvering and stimulating than men do, plus a little more time. Interestingly, some research indicates that 75 percent of women don't climax during intercourse alone, which is a shock to many men, and to many women for that matter.[10] So females need some extras. . . .

Here's the part that you're responsible for: communicating your needs, wants, and desires to your partner. Many women fake it in the beginning of a relationship, which is doing a disservice not only to your relationship but also to all womankind—how will men understand what women really need if they fake it? Remember, profiling requires being authentic and real, both in the bedroom and out.

Handled correctly, the dilemma of good chemistry accompanied by so-so sex can be overcome with communication and a partner who is willing to listen . . . and act on it. It takes time to get a feel for someone new; not only with regard to sex but also in your overall relationship. It's unrealistic to expect fabulous sex immediately. Don't profile a guy out based on so-so sex alone if the relationship in general is healthy and he is interested in making you happy.

The Dark Side of Sex

PROFILE AND PROTECT YOURSELF

IT'S PSYCHOLOGICALLY EASIER and just more fun to think about the pleasant side of sex. Of course we want to keep romance, passion, and sensuality at the forefront. Yet the reality is that somewhere in the back of our minds, knowledge about the dark side of sex is ever present. It manifests itself every time a woman worries about her health after a casual sexual encounter. It moves to the forefront every time a woman is alone with a man and feels uncomfortable or unsafe.

Profiling for the dangers that surround sex allows you to attack the fear head-on and to problem-solve rather than dismiss, deny, or hide from these thoughts and feelings. By finding the courage to face the bad stuff and deal with it, you actually make the good stuff even better. Not only will you reduce your anxiety and risk for these dangers, but you'll also be proud of yourself for addressing difficult issues. The two main issues I'm going to focus on in this chapter are sexually transmitted diseases (STDs) and date rape.

Profiling for STDs

AIDS . . . HEPATITIS B . . . HERPES . . . chlamydia . . . crabs . . . gon-
orrhea. These sexually transmitted diseases obviously don't evoke
delightful images. A woman is not going to feel romantic, sexy, or elegant asking a man if he has genital warts. Nor are herpes lesions the
best subject for polite dinner conversation with a hot date. But these
are conversations we all must have.

If you don't discuss STDs with your dates, then you may end up
discussing treatment options with your doctor. Women must take
responsibility for their health. Women have the right to take care of
their bodies and to show concern for their health.

THE STD SCREEN

Before sleeping with a man, engaging in risky sexual activities, or
deciding to dispense with condoms, you need to make sure the guy
has taken a trip to the doctor and been screened for STDs. And fair is
fair: If he's done it, you should do it for him as well.

COMMUNICATING WITH HIM ABOUT STDS

As you begin the STD discussion, you'll want to have some questions
in mind. If you feel excessively embarrassed to bring up this subject,
consider the probability that it's too early in the relationship to have
sex. If you don't have open communication about STDs, then you're
probably not going to have good communication about your sexual
needs, either.

You may want to ask the following questions as you are communicating and profiling:

- Have you ever been tested for a sexually transmitted disease?
- Have you been treated for a sexually transmitted disease?
- Have you had a lot of partners? What's your "number"?
- Have you used condoms with everyone you've slept with, every time?
- Have you ever had symptoms of STDs?
- Have any of your partners had an STD?
- Do you think and talk about these things before you have sex with a woman?

For those of you worried about getting caught up in the passion and skipping the sexual profiling, try this visualization technique: Close your eyes and picture all the little germs that could be having a party on his penis at that moment. If you're not going to profile, at least put a latex tent over that party!

A MATTER OF TRUST?

The only way to be sure he has gotten tested is if you go with him and see the test results afterward. You could offer to accompany him to his appointment or try to get back-to-back appointments so you can be tested at the same time. Some might say, "Look, buddy, I don't know you that well. I need to protect *myself*, so I need to see the results!"

In lieu of going with him or asking for proof flat-out, trust becomes a major issue. Ask yourself if he has ever lied to you before. Also take note of the way he reacts during your STD discussion. Is he caring, supportive, and open, or is he dismissive, evasive, and annoyed? Does he show concern for his health as well as yours, or does he have a reckless attitude toward both?

A worthwhile guy is going to be impressed that a woman has the self-value to bring this delicate topic to the floor. He'll also be impressed by someone who stands up for what's important. A woman who chooses to protect her health and her life is a woman who values herself and her life. This is a fabulous thing, and a fabulous man will recognize it and wallow in it.

Twenty-eight-year-old Brenda, who was going out with a rather virile, ex–football player type, was worried about bringing up the subject of STDs. She was afraid that he would balk at the idea of getting tested. What if this started a fight that would end their month-and-a-half-long relationship? In a way, she saw asking him as not only an STD test but also as a test of their relationship.

Much to Brenda's surprise, football guy passed both tests with flying colors. She was pleased to learn that he had asked his last girlfriend to get tested and that he had been good about condom use in the past. He told Brenda that he was confident about his good health and had no problem getting tested. It turned out that the guy was also really good in bed!

Of course, this is the ideal scenario. Some guys may not be so confident about their good health (all the more reason for you to be concerned!). Some guys may be scared to go to the doctor. You can be supportive and caring. If the guy is decent and willing, you can help him work through his anxiety.

Profiling for Date Rape

WHEN YOU ARE ATTRACTED TO SOMEONE, interested in someone, or agree to go out with someone, you want to be able to trust him. It's hard to think that a person you are choosing to spend time with could be dangerous, particularly if he's dangerous in a sexual way. According to U.S. Department of Justice Statistics, about 500,000 women report being raped or sexually assaulted each year.[1] Of that

500,000, 26 percent, or 130,000, were victimized by intimates, including boyfriends, ex-boyfriends, or spouses.

It's important to remember that through profiling, you have the power to reduce your chance of being a statistic and to protect yourself. By not only profiling the guy, but also profiling for dangerous situations, you can seriously reduce the risk of finding yourself in the middle of a nightmare.

WHO IS THE DATE RAPIST?

Date rapists and sexual assaulters don't necessarily have shifty eyes, nor do they sport a "bad guy" sign that makes them easy to spot. So it's important to approach every date with an air of caution. That said, researchers have identified some behaviors or attitudes that date rapists/sexual assaulters tend to have in common. Be particularly careful with a man you know who exhibits one or more of the following characteristics:

- accepts violence and aggression as a normal part of dating[2]
- exploits or ignores you and is hostile toward women in general[3]
- displays antisocial/sociopathic behavior[4]
- is callous and controlling[5]
- believes in traditional male/female sex roles and is very macho[6]
- has had either voluntary or involuntary sexual experiences at an early age[7]
- has a lot of sexual experience and a lot of varied sexual experience, for example, group sex[8]

Date Rape Watch

IN MANY PARTS OF THE COUNTRY, especially the Midwest, tornado watches and warnings are par for the course. A warning means that a tornado has already been spotted, whereas a watch means that all the conditions are right for a tornado to occur. Listed below are some favorable conditions for date rape. Keep watch for these situations so that you don't get blindsided by a dangerous whirlwind.

DATE RAPE WATCH 1

If either you, your date, or both are under the influence of drugs or alcohol there is a risk factor.[9] Date rapes are often associated with intoxication. Keep an eye out for how much your date is drinking and for signs of other substance use, such as out of-the-ordinary agitation or sedation. Also, drinking from a glass that's been left unattended is a bad idea. There are several "date rape" drugs such as Rohypnol (roofies) that could be slipped into your drink. Rohypnol debilitates a person by causing confusion and a drunklike stupor among other effects. Rohypnol can also affect the date rape victim's memory for the event, possibly causing a blackout with regard to what happened.

DATE RAPE WATCH 2

The man being in control of the date has been associated with date rape.[10] If he does all the initiating, planning, paying, and driving, it puts you in a subordinate position. Even out the power differential by assuming a key role in the dating process and sticking your two cents in.

DATE RAPE WATCH 3

If your date has gotten you in his territory or in an isolated location, you could be at risk. Realistically, you're not in harm's way sitting across the table from someone in a crowded restaurant. More isolated places are the problem. In this day and age, decent guys know this and a man with good intentions is going to keep your first dating experiences more public, or at least not get offended if you decline an offer to go to a secluded location—like back to his place.

Watch out for guys who want to "surprise" you by taking you to a location that's a secret. Also, think twice before going to an area that you're unfamiliar with. Having your own car is best, but if he's driving, have a backup transportation plan (or at least cab fare) in case things start going sour.

DATE RAPE WATCH 4

A situation in which boundaries are left undefined could lead to dangerous conclusions on the man's part. When it comes to sex, it's best to leave as little up to interpretation as possible. It's been found that date rapists tend to interpret neutral cues (a touch on his arm, laughing at his jokes) or even slightly sexual cues (a hug, a kiss on the cheek) as signs that a woman wants to have sex.[11] Moreover, studies show that miscommunication about sex is associated with date rape.[12] If you feel uncomfortable, degraded, or violated, let the guy know it's "No!"

DATE RAPE WATCH 5

If you get an undefined weird, bad feeling, pay attention. Don't knock your intuition. It comes from a very wise place. Subconsciously, you may be picking up cues that your conscious mind can't put into words yet. If you get an *eeewwww* feeling, be proud instead of embarrassed to listen to it!

DATE RAPE ON CAMPUS

According to some statistics, one out of four female college students will be raped or sexually assaulted during her college career.[13] College women need to face these numbers and take back control!

In order to understand the special circumstances that students face, the question to ask is, What distinguishes the college and university lifestyle from the world outside? Well, of course there's a lot of youth, a lot of experimentation, and a lot of need to blow off steam.

There is also the fraternity and sorority lifestyle that has become a culture unto itself. Although this brotherhood/sisterhood culture can have some wonderful aspects to it, there is also a seriously dangerous undertone. Fascinatingly, the riskiest time in terms of date rape for college women during their first year is from the day they move in until holiday break. Why? Because it's the main time for rush parties.

In order to combat this, Scott Lindquist, in *The Date Rape Prevention Book*, has included characteristics of high-risk fraternity houses and low-risk fraternity houses.[14] For all of you college women and parents of college women out there, go over the profiling techniques above and then incorporate this method of fraternity profiling into your repertoire.

High-Risk Fraternity Parties Have . . .

- more men than women or, interestingly, more women than men

- groups of men splintering off from groups of women, such as all the men drinking together by the keg
- a bunch of men disrespecting women—telling sexually inappropriate jokes, or rating women's bodies
- gross, disgusting bathrooms riddled with vomit and other unknown bodily fluids
- a cold atmosphere not conducive to smiling and laughing. Men are likely to be openly hostile and quick with put-downs, cursing, in-your-face attitudes, and too much touching
- a palpable, sexually charged atmosphere
- dancing that changes after midnight from big groups on the floor to only couples grinding
- men trying to isolate women so they can put the moves on
- men bragging about how many women they've just done

Compared to this, the low-risk parties are going to sound like a great time. Still, it's important not to be lulled into a false sense of security anywhere!

Low-Risk Fraternity Parties Have . . .

- about the same number of men and women
- a welcoming atmosphere with friendly interaction between men and women
- couples dancing as well as people dancing in groups
- many couples at the party who are in relationships and are affectionate with each other
- several people who seem to already know one another
- a polite tone; if there is pushing or shoving, the people involved tend to apologize
- clean bathrooms that have toilet paper and soap

Be Angry, Not Embarrassed

Always remember that you don't have to apologize for being cautious. If a man makes you feel as if you do, then get angry and even more wary, not embarrassed. A man who doesn't care about your health and safety is not worthwhile.

Another important idea to take from this chapter is to deal with these issues, but then let them go. It does no good to dwell on them and live in a constant state of fear. So go ahead and be your fun, spontaneous self, just don't forget to serve it up with a side of your profiling instincts.

Last, if you are currently dealing with the aftermath of date rape or an STD, it's important to do some self-profiling. Have you dealt with these issues by getting the proper attention from medical and mental-health professionals? Have you examined how these experiences could impact your present relationship or future relationships?

Commitment-Ready Men versus Commitment-Phobic Men

LEARN HOW TO *NOT* GET USED!

NO ONE LIKES BEING USED. No one wants to suffer through being played. It can leave you feeling tricked, manipulated, mistreated, and uncared for, besides wreaking havoc with you self-worth. Profiling can help you guard against being taken advantage of by the opposite sex. Here are ways to profile a man for commitment readiness.

The Road to Nowhere

FOR MOST WOMEN, the primary topic that comes to mind when they're talking about themselves or someone else being "used" is sex. Take Rachel, a twenty-four-year-old graduate student who fell hard for Dillon, a charming twenty-nine-year-old architect. After about three months of heavy dating and a lot of sex, Dillon called it quits and squashed Rachel's heart in the process.

Going over and over the situation in her mind, Rachel couldn't figure out how she misread the relationship in such a major way. It seemed as if he really cared. He alluded to future events like taking a trip to his parents' house together, as well as signing up for dancing lessons. Was Dillon dating her to honestly see if they were a compatible couple, or did he see her only as a brief fling? In her gut, Rachel had the feeling it was the latter.

Tired of being obsessed with the question, a month after the breakup, she confronted Dillon point-blank, asking him, "Did you play me?" He didn't answer yes, but didn't say no either. Then he made reference to how great their physical relationship was. So according to him, she really had nothing to complain about.

Rather than giving Rachel the closure she was seeking, Dillon's rather cold response turned her stomach. Now, every time she dates a guy, she compulsively looks for the Dillon inside him, which has become an unhealthy self-fulfilling prophecy for her.

Being used for sex by a guy can have even more serious consequences than the remaining indignation. Women have to worry not only about the emotional repercussions but also the physical ones. Who wants to be left with an STD as a parting gift from a player?

Use Me Up

SOME WOMEN MAY THINK that if the boundaries are clearly defined and each person's cards are laid on the table, then it's okay for you "to use me while I use you." In some cases it could turn out okay, but the problem is that this can be a dangerous game no matter how clear the definition of the relationship. Thirty-two-year-old Sean found this out the hard way after his relationship with forty-one-year-old Ronda ended. Both knew their relationship couldn't work long-term from the start because of conflicting ideas about having a family. Sean didn't want children, and Ronda was interested in adopting.

The problem was that divergent goals don't necessarily negate fiery chemistry, which the two of them definitely had. So as a sort of middle ground, they agreed to have an exclusive relationship for three months only. Ronda was fine with this relationship deadline, as was Sean—until the last week started drawing near. At the end, Sean felt more empty and hurt than he had bargained for.

The best way to treat these kinds of casual relationships is cautiously. Be careful that neither you nor your partner is mistreating or exploiting the other. Open communication about expectations for the relationship is a must. Moreover, be aware regarding the frequency of these noncommittal interactions. A chronic and pervasive pattern of them could (but not necessarily) signal some self-esteem issues or other serious mental-health issues that have not been dealt with yet, such as a history of sexual abuse.

Emotional Use and Abuse

SEX ISN'T THE ONLY THING women can be used for, because sex isn't the only thing women have to offer. Think of all the support you may give to a man: comfort when he's hurting, reassurance when he's down on himself, and an empathic ear when he needs someone to listen. You also may do a lot of practical things for a man, such as helping to create a clean and cozy home environment and helping to pay the bills.

Unfortunately, some men are willing or even expect to take these things from women without giving much back. For this type of guy, women exist only to fulfill their needs. They squeeze out every last ounce they can from their current girlfriend, but when she's dry and can't give any more, they move on to the next without hesitation.

Many times, you can spot these guys talking about what their girlfriends do *for them* as opposed to their girlfriends' inner qualities, which they barely notice. Forty-year-old pharmaceutical rep Steve is a good example. When talking about his current girlfriend, he stated, "It's really nice to have something to do every Friday night, ya know? I come home from work and I don't have to worry about making plans because I'll be hangin' out with her." Absent is any acknowledgment of her special characteristics, including a vivacious personality and fun-loving spirit.

Miguel's story has the same theme but a different plot. Always worried about being perceived as gay because he's fifty and not married, Miguel likes to have a woman around as his arm ornament for work functions and other "couplish" social events. He often thinks, "Man, it's great to have Kathy around when I have one of those damn things to go to. . . . I hate going by myself. Next week's my high school reunion, and I'm not having everyone thinking I'm gay."

It can be especially tricky when a guy is using you for emotional support. Because he seems so puppy-doggish and vulnerable, he may appear to be sensitive. He probably is—sensitive about *his* own emotions but not others' feelings. Soon the realization comes with regard to how much time and energy you spend on healing his wounds. Worse, there's no even exchange; this man has no support or commitment to give back to you.

A perfect example is Shane, a thirty-four-year-old recently separated optometrist. His wife began having an affair with the neighbor because she felt neglected by her overworked, hard-playing, and very inattentive husband. Shane's self-esteem was smashed by his wife's infidelity, and because he felt very possessive of her, he became completely focused on winning her back.

But Shane couldn't go through the process alone, so that's where Donna came in. Poor unsuspecting Donna, who thought Shane was completely taken with her, fell into the role of emotional doormat.

Whenever he needed to complain about how wronged he was by his wife, Donna was there. Whenever he chose to vent his hurt feelings, Donna was there. Whenever he needed her for physical comfort, Donna was there.

Donna did a fantastic job of propping Shane back up again. He was almost as good as new. So good, in fact, that when he won his wife back he discarded Donna without a blink of an eye.

Shapes and Sizes of Commitment

DONNA'S SITUATION, of course, is a clear-cut case of someone being emotionally used and abused. Anecdotal evidence suggests that when an exploitative relationship such as this one ends, women tend to feel worse than when a nonexploitative one ends. After the exploitive relationships, women tend to ask themselves questions:

- How could I have wasted so much time and effort on someone who treated me like that?
- How stupid am I?
- How could I let myself get taken advantage of in that way?
- Why didn't I see it?
- He didn't care about me at all, did he? And I stayed with him all that time!
- What is wrong with me that he couldn't truly care about me?

This is potentially damaging self-talk that can take a toll on self-esteem. In contrast, women whose nonexploitative relationships have ended seem to strike a different tone. When women feel that their former partners had similar commitment goals, together with a sincere interest in getting to know them, they tend to make comments such as:

- We both tried, but it just didn't work out.
- I didn't feel the chemistry for him.
- My goals and his goals were totally separate.
- We both started realizing we weren't compatible and didn't want to waste each other's time.
- I miss him and it hurts like hell, but if I had it to do over again, I would. . . . It was a good try.

Notice how these statements are less self-punishing? That's what comes from two partners who have given each other a fair shot at making a relationship work. It's still not pleasant to break up, yet it's a whole lot less damaging to our pride if our perspective is one of having been equal partners who put equal effort into a situation that just didn't happen to work out.

It's important to remember that just because you didn't end up at the altar doesn't mean that your relationship was exploitive or unhealthy. Healthy relationships exist between couples focused on their careers, couples with children from prior relationships, as well as senior couples. They may enjoy companionship and emotional support without the rigorous commitment of marriage.

Relationships in today's society come in a variety of wonderful, healthy shapes and sizes. What's even more wonderful is that you can determine the level of commitment that *you* want! No one can force you to commit to someone if you don't want to, nor can he push you into a situation in which you feel used. That's where the power of profiling for commitment lies: The decision is in your hands.

What Exactly Is Commitment, and Is He Feeling It?

MANY WOMEN ARE INTERESTED in finding a relationship with a deep level of commitment—one that has a future and will eventually lead to marriage. So let's explore this concept of commitment further and learn how to tell if he's feeling it.

Thus far commitment has been defined by what it is *not*; among other things, "getting used" is definitely not commitment. But now let's define commitment by what it is.[1]

Commitment Means . . .

- having the "intention to persist" in the relationship
- being psychologically attached to each other
- developing the "cognitive orientation" that "yes, we're in this for the long term"

HONORABLE INTENTIONS

If a man has the intention to persist in the relationship, it means that he is goal-directed, and the goal is you! If you look for it with open eyes, without bias, you can see when intention is truly in his actions. He makes the effort to be with you, attend to you, and, in general, integrate you into his life.

A man without intention is easy to spot. You get the feeling of aimlessness and lack of purpose in the relationship. Twenty-five-year-old CJ got this sense a few times from men she called her "activity guys." These men were so filled to the brim with hobbies and activities that the *intention* was to fit CJ into their schedules, not to make CJ the emotional center. Now she always cautions, "Beware of the activity guys!"

If you are sensing this kind of relationship aimlessness with your boyfriend, it may be time to have a talk. Let him know what your intentions are and find out whether or not he wants to match them.

PSYCHOLOGICAL ATTACHMENT

Psychological attachment is very important because the majority of men are essentially needy creatures, and they need women. They don't tend to build the kind of intricate emotional support networks that women do. When they finally choose to attach to someone, they often fall hard and deep.

Remember this when you feel depressed over the fact that there seem to be fewer commitment-oriented men. No matter what, there are always going to be men out there who need you very much! By profiling for them, you'll find what you're looking for.

What exactly are they psychologically attaching to? To name just a few things, men become accustomed to caring and intimacy, the sexual chemistry you have together, the empathic understanding that goes both ways, and the history that you begin to share. Most important, when it's special and right, men psychologically attach to that which is uniquely you!

On the other hand, you may have developed a strong attachment that is not reciprocated. It's happened to everyone, and it is terrible when it does. Did you ever feel like you tried to force an emotional bond that wasn't there?

Just as attachments are multifaceted and somewhat mysterious, disconnections are complicated as well. There are "everyday sociopaths" and narcissists (to be discussed in subsequent chapters) out there who are entirely unable to have a healthy, in-depth psychological attachment to another human being. Nothing short of a miracle can change these men. To try and do so is the equivalent of banging your head against a brick wall.

A host of psychological issues, including post-traumatic stress, depression, and obsessive-compulsive personality characteristics, can factor into the inability to attach. However, if a man is motivated to seek and get the help he needs, the possibility of developing healthy attachments can exist despite psychological issues.

Last, there is always that other possibility that women don't want to face. A man's lack of psychological attachment to us may not have anything to do with his "issues": It may mean he's not in love.

This is one of the hardest things in life to accept, but by profiling, you *can* swallow it! Through the process of profiling, you more easily learn to realize and accept reality. With this knowledge, it's possible to move forward by creating better relationships for yourself, rather than staying stuck in the same old stale fantasies.

THOUGHTS OF COMMITMENT

When a man is commitment-ready, his brain is in commitment mode. His cognitive orientation is that of a person who is planning for a future of togetherness. In his mind, you're perceived not only as an activity partner or a sex partner but also a life partner. Thoughts and statements begin to turn to "we" and "us" instead of "I" and "me." There is a shift from the duality of two toward the unity of one.

A man who doesn't have the cognitive commitment orientation still has the thought process of single guy, although it may manifest in different ways. For example, he might seem to have a one-track career focus, or he might display an immature thought process that is heavily weighted toward self-gratification.

Pay attention to his words in order to find out his cognitive commitment orientation. This includes the words that he purposefully says to you, as well as words that come out in casual conversations.

Eventually, his thoughts about your future together will emerge—intentionally or unintentionally.

Why Men Won't Commit

HOW OFTEN HAVE YOU and your friends sat around discussing the reasons why men won't commit? Tackling the reasons why men won't commit can lead you in the direction of a man who will—if that's what you choose. Here's some research you can add to your discussion.

The National Marriage Project, based at Rutgers University, undertook a study that included sixty single, heterosexual men, ages twenty-five to thirty-three.[2] Although the men were from a variety of backgrounds, they all came from major metropolitan areas: northern New Jersey, Chicago, Washington, DC, and Houston. Most of the participants had some college or higher, and their incomes were $21,000 and above.

The really good news is that these men said they would like to get married and have families eventually; the bad news is that they're not necessarily in a hurry.

The Top Ten Reasons Why Men Won't Commit

1. Sex outside of marriage is readily available.

2. Living together provides the benefits of marriage without the commitment.

3. They're scared of divorce and its financial implications.

4. They don't want to have children until they're older.

5. They worry about the changes and compromises that come with marriage.

6. Their soul mate hasn't made an appearance yet and they're still waiting.

7. Today there aren't as many social pressures to marry.

8. They are hesitant to marry a woman who has children by another man.

9. They want to buy a house first.

10. They want to revel in singlehood for as long as possible.

Take a look at some of these reasons in more detail and how you can use them to your advantage when profiling for commitment.

SEX

The National Marriage Project found that woman's intuition has always been correct: When a man is interested in a long-term relationship, he is more likely to wait for sex. In fact, 74 percent of these single men want to get to know a woman before they sleep with her, *if* they are really interested. To the men, holding off on sex usually meant until the fourth or fifth date; however, one man in the study waited seven months.

Of course, the study also showed that casual sex or one-night stands elicit an anticommitment reaction in men. They reported being less "respectful" and less "interested" in a real relationship with a woman who would go to bed with them right away.

What does all this mean for women seeking a long-term relationship? It means that one of the easiest ways to determine if a guy is really interested is to hold off on sex. If he pushes too hard or stops calling after the word "no," you've just done a great job of weeding out someone who probably isn't ready to commit.

Jim, a thirty-two-year-old restaurant owner, told his girlfriend, "I don't want to push you into sex because I don't want to push you away." The line may be a little bit cheesy, but he meant it. When she was ready to make sex part of the relationship a couple of months later, Jim promptly fulfilled her request to get an HIV test, showing that he cared about her health and well-being. Now, this is a guy interested in commitment!

DOES LIVE-IN GIRLFRIEND EQUAL BRIDE-TO-BE?

The prospect of living with a man needs to be carefully weighed by women who maintain marriage as their goal. Clearly, according to the National Marriage Project study, when living together, men enjoy getting a lot of the benefits of marriage without having to say "I do."

For some women, the pros of living together outweigh the cons. Many women wouldn't think of marrying a man before a good test drive around the shared living space. Yet for others who are seeking that legal piece of paper, living together first may not always be the best option. The probability that living together will lead to marriage after three years is 58 percent; after five years it jumps to 70 percent.[3]

Your interpretation of these stats is going to depend a lot on your perspective. Some will look at these numbers and say, "Not bad. If I live with him three years, then my odds of getting married are better than fifty–fifty!"

Others will say, "I have to live with him for three long years and then have a 42 percent chance of *not* getting married!" If you're saying this to yourself, then you're also more likely to be concerned by the fact that those who live together before a first marriage are more likely to get divorced or separated than those who do not.[4]

One word of caution about living together: Some men use the live-in situation to bide their time until the arrival of someone better. Some of the men in the National Marriage Project study said that they have lower standards for live-in girlfriends; sometimes men see them as their okay-for-now women until they come across the person they really want to be with for life.

MEN: COWARDLY LIONS WHEN IT COMES TO CHANGE AND COMPROMISE?

Men worry about the changes and compromises that come with marriage; largely this is due to men fearing their loss of independence. Who better to exemplify this than one of the most famous commitment-phobic characters of all time, *Sex and the City*'s Mr. Big, played by Chris Noth? The elusive, on-again, off-again relationship that Big developed with Carrie tried and tested her patience, at times to the point of a breakdown.

You could see it in Big's eyes—the trapped animal looking for a way out of its cage—every time Carrie threatened his autonomy by getting too close emotionally. Interestingly, it might have been not only a lack of will to give up his independence but also a lack of faith in himself to make the changes and compromises that are necessary for every healthy relationship. Fortunately for Carrie, Big eventually developed the confidence in his ability to have a healthy relationship and realized that the good of love outweighs the risks.

How do you know if you're dating a man who, despite kicking and screaming along the way, is willing to trade some independence for some interdependence? Two of the best ways are to take a look at how he has dealt with change and compromise in the past, as well as how he does so in the present with you. If his history includes less change than you have in your pocket, be afraid! If finding the middle ground consistently turns into a bloody battleground, be very afraid!

LOVE ME, LOVE MY CHILD!

Women with children (or those contemplating single parenthood) may be concerned that men may be hesitant to marry when there is a child involved. Do not get discouraged! Through profiling, you can increase your odds of meeting men who see motherhood as an asset.

Thirty-five-year-old Gia made a great connection with a man online after she read his profile and found that he was a single father looking for a single mother to whom he could relate. To connect with people who identify with and relate to being a single parent, it's also a good idea to look toward clubs and organizations, such as Parents Without Partners, that cater to single moms and dads.

No matter what, always keep in mind that a man who is deeply fond of a woman is apt to develop a fondness for her offspring, because a man who is very interested in a woman tends to be interested in everything about her.

Can I Improve My Chances of Getting Married?

THE NATIONAL MARRIAGE PROJECT's study on commitment has given us a good sneak peek into the male psyche. Let's take a minute to revisit the good news. Many men, just like many women, eventually want committed relationships! Even a study of college students backs this up. What's intriguing is that students of both sexes believed men were less likely to be interested in commitment; yet, when asked, men expressed just as much interest in committed relationships as women.[5]

Neil Chethik, author of *VoiceMale*, tells us that one of the main reasons the men he surveyed married was simply that they "like company." They wanted the "physical, emotional, and intellectual companionship" a woman can provide. Yet it wasn't only the touchy-feely stuff that finally got men to the altar. Chethik states that practical reasons, such as wanting to start a family or perhaps a work-related relocation, often served as that final push. There is a very logical, matter-of-fact, and gradual side to men's decision-making process when it comes to the *m* word.[6]

For many, however, a gradual or eventual relationship is not good enough; some want a committed relationship *now*! How can women improve their chances immediately? Well, for one thing, although there is less social pressure to marry today, some still exists—this goes for men as well as women. If a guy's friends are into marriage, he's probably more likely to take the plunge himself. When you're profiling for commitment, profile his friends too. If he's hanging out with a group of confirmed bachelors, it may be a signal that he's not ready for his single days to end.

Let's turn our attention to location, location, location. All the men who served as research guinea pigs in the National Marriage Project study are from major metropolitan areas. The fact is that women are less likely to marry by age thirty in metropolitan areas than in nonmetropolitan areas. Furthermore, the chance of getting married by thirty is worst in central cities and best in nonmetropolitan areas.[7] In order to improve your odds, start shopping the burbs or, maybe better yet, rural America. Even if you're a confirmed city dweller, online dating now makes it much easier to meet people outside your immediate area.

Keep in mind that a guy who owns his own home may be putting out the ready-for-marriage signal. The underlying message of home ownership is that he's financially stable and perhaps ready to help shoulder the responsibilities that come with a family.

Showing that you are financially independent will alleviate some of his fears regarding the monetary implications of marriage and . . . divorce. Remember, he's probably worried that all his money will disappear in the event of a divorce. Lessen that fear with signs of your own financial security, such as stable employment, money management skills, and perhaps home ownership.

Many men in the National Marriage Project study said that they were waiting to commit because they were waiting for their soul mate. The idea of finding a "soul mate" can be beautiful as long as it is also realistic.

Men often complain about women who are looking for an ideal prince charming, because what man could to live up to that fantasy? Unfortunately, some men are guilty of the same syndrome: They're looking for a heavenly angel, not an earthly woman. Therefore, they postpone and postpone commitment because they are waiting for perfection to walk through the door. Well, it's not gonna happen.

By finding a man with realistic expectations about women and relationships, you'll find a man with a mind-set for marriage. This guy is much more likely to weather the hard times with you, because he expects them and prepares for them. He wants to work things out with you rather than escaping to another relationship. He's not always looking for a better deal. If you find that you are with a man who is perpetually looking for something better to come along, look for something better yourself.

COMMITMENT FACTS

The following are a few random commitment facts to add to your arsenal:

- The amount of time between divorce and remarriage seems to be dropping from an average of five years to three years.[8]
- Attractive people are less likely to have a marriage that lasts, perhaps because they have easier access to enticing alternatives.[9]

- In one study, 21 percent of engaged women over forty met their fiancés at clubs directed toward physical activities, such as gyms and ski, swim, and bicycling clubs.[10]
- There's a real possibility that a man who has had one or more long-term relationships without marrying is a "stringer," meaning that he could be a perpetual serial monogamist.[11]
- Forty-seven percent of husbands surveyed said that it took them at least a year from the time they met to decide they wanted to marry their future wives.[12]
- Thirty-eight percent of women surveyed who went online looking for "a serious relationship" are now either in a committed relationship or are married to a man they met in cyberspace.[13]

Commitment-Ready vs. Commitment-Phobic

AFTER TAKING ALL this information into consideration, it's easy to see that commitment-ready men behave significantly differently toward women than commitment-phobic men. The table below boils down the qualities of each so you can spot them right away.

COMMITMENT-READY PROFILE	COMMITMENT-PHOBIC PROFILE
He pursues you.	You pursue him.
You're priority #1.	You're priority #11, #25, or #48.

He initiates spending time with you.	You initiate spending time with him.
Cares about your well-being.	Cares only about his own well-being.
Attentive.	Inattentive.
Interested in what interests you.	Interested in what interests him.
Watches videos with you when you're sick.	Takes off when you're sick.
Plans ahead and is consistent.	Calls at the last minute and is sporadic.
Focuses on "catching you."	Focuses on "the chase."
Invests in you.	Sees you as a cost.
Focuses on the future.	Focuses on "the now."
Advances the relationship.	Stalls the relationship.
Says he's committed and acts committed.	Says he's committed and acts indifferent.
Likes face-to-face contact.	Likes e-mails and text messaging.

Doesn't have much need for excuses.	Always has an excuse.
Prefers "couple time."	Prefers "out-with-the-boys" time.
Gets to know your friends and family.	Keeps his posse separate from you.
Has all his ducks in a row.	Is totally loosey-goosey.

Keep in mind that the amount of time you've been seeing a guy factors into some of the commitment-ready and commitment-phobic profiles. Obviously, you don't want to be his number one priority after the first date. The point is that some of these commitment characteristics will be evident right away, whereas you'll have to see how the others grow and develop.

Should I Stay or Should I Bolt?

IF THE MAN you're interested in has many commitment-ready qualities, you're probably thinking, "Great, I'm in good shape." Regrettably, a lot of women either have, or will have, strong feelings for the commitment-phobic guy. The next logical question is, "How long do I stick it out with a man who isn't ready to commit to me?" And then, of course, there's the issue of will he *ever* actually be ready?

Obviously, the answers to these questions aren't simple. Each case is individualized and must be taken on its own merit. However, keep in mind a couple of guidelines when you're wondering, "Should I stay or should I bolt?"

First and foremost, you need to look at what's best for you! That means keeping your options open. If you feel that you can't break away from a commitment-phobic guy because you're in love with him, that's one thing. But making a commitment to him by being exclusive is another. It's important to evaluate the level of commitment you are affording him versus the level of commitment he is offering you.

If you're dating a commitment-phobic guy, there is nothing wrong with letting him know that you're keeping one eye open, which means keeping your possibilities open. The flip side is keeping both eyes shut to new opportunities and to perhaps a better situation for you.

Another idea to tuck away in the back of your mind is the tug-of-war aspect to this commitment-phobic game. In reality, you probably have as good a chance of convincing him to get married as he has of convincing you not to get married. By thinking of it this way, it's easier to see how hard you will have to pull the rope in order to change his mind. Remember, he's pulling for bachelorhood as hard as you're pulling for marriage. That's why this tug-of-war can often get stalled, making it harder and harder to hang on and less and less worth the effort. If this is the way you're beginning to feel, a whole new game may be an exciting and timely answer.

Discovering
Mr. Self-Actualized

IF WE ARE NOT CAREFUL, it can be too easy for us to fall into a pattern of constantly criticizing men. How many times have you said to yourself, "All men are scum" or "All guys are players—they only want one thing"? Negative stereotyping starts to pop up after a few bad experiences with a few badly behaved men.

However, by jumping to the conclusion that all men are evil, a woman's perception of reality becomes negatively skewed. Even where there's good to be found, you see only bad. The glass is more than half empty. The problem is that if you anticipate negative behavior, in the end, that's all you're going to find.

So what are the good qualities in men that you should be looking for? As it happens, the well-known psychologist Abraham Maslow has given us pretty good guidelines to this question.[1] The good guy is no other than Mr. Self-Actualized!

Mr. Self-Actualized can be defined as a man who freely expresses his inner nature and works toward fulfilling his potential. Mr. Self-Actualized is continuously working toward being a better man.

Following are the top ten characteristics of Mr. Self-Actualized based on Maslow's definition of self-actualized people. Keep in mind that Maslow talked about the idea of self-actualization in terms of both men and women, but for the purposes of profiling I'm just going to talk about Mr. rather than Ms.

The Top Ten Characteristics of Mr. Self-Actualized

1. creative

2. perceptive

3. independent

4. curious

5. warm

6. ethical

7. humble

8. open

9. funny

10. able to enjoy "peak experiences"

As you have probably figured out, Mr. Self-Actualized is a rare gem. In fact, Maslow himself estimated that less than 1 percent of individuals are actually self-actualized.

If there are only a few of them around in real life, Mr. Self-Actualized turns up in fiction all the time. Think of the heroes and good guys in your favorite books, movies, and TV shows. More

than likely these guys have a few Mr. Self-Actualized characteristics.

In contrast to the emotionally distant Mr. Big, Aidan Shaw is a
fantastic example of a fictional self-actualizer. This guy lasted a while
as Carrie Bradshaw's love interest. But what made him so special?

*Aidan Shaw—furniture designer, dog owner, guy with a country
cabin—he's the perfect opposite to the commitment-phobic, hard-
to-pin-down Mr. Big. Aidan is so warm and accessible and
THERE for Carrie. He even refinishes her floors and makes her a
home-cooked meal.*[2]

This is not to say that Aidan was a wimp by any means. He was always able to stand up to Carrie and let his needs be known (fidelity,
for starters). But even with all of Aidan's self-actualizing potential,
he still was not able to win the girl's heart. At the end of the series,
Carrie wound up with a new and improved Big.

Anyone who "profiled" Aidan and Carrie as a couple saw im-
pending doom from the outset because they were incompatible on so
many levels. Still, this fictional Mr. Self-Actualized has it in him to
make some other fictional female very, very happy!

In terms of real people, Maslow included Abraham Lincoln,
Thomas Jefferson, and Albert Einstein as likely self-actualizers.

But what about a contemporary and hot *real* Mr. Self-Actualized?
Of course, without actually knowing someone, there's much more
guesswork involved, but as far as public persona goes, singer/enter-
tainer Nick Lachey is a great example of Mr. Self-Actualized.

Lachey is that rare fabulous paradox of the sensitive manly man,
the buff jock who is not afraid to show emotions metaphorically
through his music or tangibly by shedding real tears. But maybe
most important, he is a good guy who is willing to admit to a more

complex self—even longing for people to see that his more complex self includes darker emotions common to all humanity.[3] Self-actualizers are not above human feelings like anger and frustration.

As you consider the ten characteristics of Mr. Self-Actualized, think of men you know who exemplify some of these qualities. Many men may have some but not all of the Mr. Self-Actualized traits, which is great and something to pay attention to because self-actualization is a process. The completely self-actualized male is rare, but keep your eye out for a great work in progress.

It's important not to turn looking for Mr. Self-Actualized into looking for Mr. Perfect. That's like chasing the holy grail—an exercise in futility. However, expecting a mate to have some of these characteristics to some degree seems like a *perfectly* reasonable expectation.

CREATIVE

Mr. Self-Actualized is a creative guy. This doesn't necessarily mean that he's an artist, a filmmaker, or a writer. Creative in this sense indicates that the guy has an imagination—that he's inventive. You might be able to find a creative accountant or an athlete with imagination.

Maslow talked about creativity as a kind of "permission to be ourselves, to fantasize, to let loose, and to be crazy, privately."[4] In other words, there's something one-of-a-kind about this guy and how he expresses himself to the world. Keep your eyes open, as his uniqueness and creativity could come to the surface in a number of ways: through his work, hobbies, sense of style, sense of humor or, better yet, through his relationship with you! How wonderful is it to be with a man who has a crazy-free imagination that matches your own crazy-free creativity?

PERCEPTIVE

Playing games with Mr. Self-Actualized is not a good idea! He is so perceptive that he can spot game players a mile away. Not only is he able easily to detect phonies, but Mr. Self-Actualized also has a deep aversion to them. Anyone who doesn't convey her true thoughts and opinions to him, or isn't able to express her real feelings, won't get far with this guy.

Playing hard to get is probably one of the worst mistakes to make with Mr. Self-Actualized. So throw out all those little strategies, like pretending you like him less than you do or pretending to be unavailable. Remember, those who play games are going to attract other game players, not Mr. Self-Actualized.

But what makes him so insightful about people? How is he able to look at the world and see things for what they really are? For one thing, he doesn't have a personality disorder that skews his perceptions. In many cases, the mentally unhealthy are hard-pressed to see anything but "themselves." A big, bloated me can get in the way of accurately seeing you, we, us, or they.

Mr. Self-Actualized is also a pretty smart guy. He has some brain power that helps him to have a shrewd understanding about what's going on around him.

INDEPENDENT

Mr. Self-Actualized tends to be an independent guy who needs his alone time, which is a daunting characteristic for some women. But the thing to keep in mind with Mr. Self-Actualized is that he's not doing it to keep you out or to push you away. Instead, his desire for his own "space" comes from his need to focus, self-reflect, and be true to who he is, which does *not* mean he has no need for a woman in his life.

If you find yourself dating a guy who has a lot of Mr. Self-Actualized's qualities, including the need for independence, allow him some solitude. By giving him his freedom and showing your own independence, you're liable to win major girlfriend points. On the other hand, if he's using the "space" excuse to the degree that you feel like you're being strung along, you may not be dealing with Mr. Self-Actualized after all. See Chapter 6, "Commitment-Ready Men vs. Commitment-Phobic Men: Learn How to *Not* Get Used!"

CURIOUS

You know the saying, Curiosity killed the cat. Well, not this cat. For him, exercising his curiosity is revitalizing. He likes to ask questions, learn about new things, and look at problems from different angles. It's as though he has an enduring sense of wonder about the world. When you're with him, you get the impression that he's engaged and not bored or ho-hum about life.

You also notice that he's curious about you. He sees you with a fresh eye and appreciates the unique and special person that you are. Don't worry about him blurring you together with the other women he has dated.

Another nice thing about his curious nature is that he's never intimidated by how smart you are. In fact, bringing up topics or viewpoints that are new to him can be a big turn-on for Mr. Self-Actualized.

WARM

Need someone to melt your cold and bruised heart? Sounds like a job for Mr. Self-Actualized! No one is more affectionate and fiery than this guy. The very look in his eyes will invite you in. . . .

Interestingly, Maslow says that self-actualizers are able to achieve "more fusion, greater love, more perfect identification, more obliteration of the ego boundaries than other people would consider possible."[5] In other words, Mr. Self-Actualized needs deep love and knows how to give it.

Not surprisingly, he's also very picky about whom he shares his time with. You're more likely to find Mr. Self-Actualized with a smaller group of close friends than a larger group of casual acquaintances. Also not surprisingly, he tends to attract a lot of attention and draw a lot of admirers even though he's not seeking it out. Don't worry. If you're interested in attracting him, just give him a sneak peek of some of your Ms. Self-Actualized traits.

ETHICAL

Mr. Self-Actualized has a sense of justice, of fairness, of right and wrong. He is a good man, yet he strives to be a better man. His sensitivity to the suffering of others provides a basis for his principles that may at times go against the conventional values of the general population. When Mr. Self-Actualized sees injustice being done, he has the courage to fight it.

An important distinction to make, however, is the truly ethical man versus Petty-Anal Guy. The truly ethical man focuses on important big-picture moral issues, whereas Petty-Anal Guy is more interested in pointing fingers and calling other people sinners. Check out these other differences between the two:

Truly Ethical Man	Petty-Anal Guy
flexible thinking	black-and-white thinking
likes to have a healthy dialogue	likes to preach
includes people	excludes people
picks his battles	nitpicks about everything
acknowledges his flaws	behaves hypocritically

HUMBLE

Mr. Self-Actualized doesn't strut around thinking he's all *that*. Instead, there's an air of quiet humility about him. In a relationship with him, you get the impression that he respects you and is able to compromise. Men who are modest rather than arrogant tend to be less controlling and more democratic in their decision making. Therefore, you are on equal footing with Mr. Self-Actualized, not in a subservient role.

This in no way implies that Mr. Self-Actualized is a meek mush ball or a wimp. Actually, he is more confident and comfortable with himself than the norm. A man who is comfortable and confident has no need to disrespect or degrade others. He has much more fun seeing what he can learn from them.

OPEN

Take a moment to think back on your previous dates and pick out the guys who you feel were less than open. They may not have actually lied to you, but they may have been guarded. Maybe the thing that tipped you off was the careful way one man always measured his words; perhaps he adopted a plastic, salesmanlike demeanor, or he may have said and done everything so perfectly that you knew something must be boiling underneath.

The good news is that Mr. Self-Actualized doesn't have to hide his true self. His conversations with you are spontaneous because there is no reason for him to calculate what he is going to say—he doesn't have a hidden agenda. You probably notice an effortlessness and easy openness in his behavior that you can't quite put your finger on.

This is not to say that all Mr. Self-Actualized thinks about are sugarplums and lollypops. He's human and has sexual drives as well as natural aggression; it's just that he's comfortable with his range of instincts and emotions and is able to be natural and unashamed of who he is.

FUNNY

If you ask one of your female friends the top five qualities she wants in a man, sense of humor will undoubtedly be on the list. It seems that most women need some frequent funny bone tickling to get through the day. However, Mr. Self-Actualized doesn't tickle you in just any old way.

For one thing, you never catch him making vicious jokes at the expense of others. He never ruthlessly digs at, degrades, or humiliates people to get a laugh. His humor elicits uninhibited laughter in you rather than making you feel withdrawn or uncomfortable, like some over-the-top racially and sexually inappropriate jokes can do.

Also, you're not likely to catch Mr. Self-Actualized with a red rubber nose and funny glasses—he's not above slapstick humor, but his brand of humor tends to run a little deeper and be a bit more philosophical. He gets how ironic life can be with all the absurd things that happen to us, and he knows that sometimes the best medicine is to sit back and laugh!

ABLE TO ENJOY "PEAK EXPERIENCES"

In order to get a taste of the ecstasy and wondrousness that life can provide, you need to have what Maslow calls "peak experiences," which are the joyful "aha" moments of life.[6] They are those moments when you are so absorbed in what you are doing or seeing that you lose all sense of time and space. For some it's an incomparable state of ecstasy; for others, it's a rapture so profound it leaves you awestruck.

Reading over the description of peak experiences probably triggered some memory flashes of aha instances in your own life. Don't feel embarrassed if the first thing you thought of was sex, because making love and being in love are often listed by people as major instigators of peak experiences. Delectable food, music, art, children, and religion are also often cited as triggers for peak experiences.

Mr. Self-Actualized knows how to let himself enjoy a peak experience. He's prone to the state of being that allows a person to be engrossed in and captivated by something. If you are lucky and persistent in your profiling, that something or *someone* could be you!

What He Needs to Become Self-Actualized

MASLOW NOT ONLY CODIFIED the characteristics of self-actualization, he described a diagram of the hierarchy of needs that should be met in order to achieve a self-actualized state of being.[7]

Maslow's Hierarchy of Needs

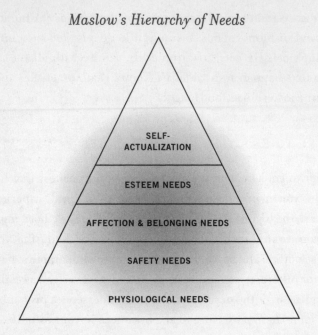

SELF-ACTUALIZATION

ESTEEM NEEDS

AFFECTION & BELONGING NEEDS

SAFETY NEEDS

PHYSIOLOGICAL NEEDS

The need hierarchy is important because in order to become Mr. Self-Actualized, a man must satisfy certain other needs first. Number one on the list is taking care of the physiological basics—food, water, sleep, and sex. Second, the guy has to meet his needs of being safe and secure. It's hard to work on being Mr. Self-Actualized if you're dodging bullets or immersed in some kind of catastrophe.

This is where you come in: A man needs affection and wants to feel like he belongs. While he could get his affection and sense of belonging from loving parents, siblings, or close friends, to really get him working through the self-actualization process he could use a little of your tenderness. Keep in mind that the making love part of sex belongs to this need level, whereas the pure animal desire to do it belongs to the physiological need level.

Last, but not least, a man needs to respect himself and feel the respect of others. He may get this through accomplishments at work or personal hobbies and interests. By achieving the goals he sets for himself, a man grows his self-esteem. Remember, this does not mean he develops a big head, just a healthy sense of self.

Finally, after these four basic needs are met, our man is ready to fulfill his potential; he is ready to work on becoming the best self he can be.

If you're able to gauge where a guy is on this need hierarchy, it will tell you a lot about him and where his priorities lie. You may also be able to tell if you have a diamond in the rough . . . perhaps he hasn't reached Mr. Self-Actualized status yet but he is well on his way. On the other hand, if you're dating a thirty-five-year-old guy whose main goal in life is to satisfy his physiological need for getting laid, it's highly unlikely that he will suddenly become enlightened and start moving up the need hierarchy.

Because self-actualization is a process, you will want to give younger guys a little more leeway. As they're trying to establish themselves in the world, they are working their way up on the need hierarchy. In these cases, look for characteristics of Mr. Self-Actualized, like morality, warmth, and creativity, which give you a good indication of their potential.

What Are My Needs?

TAKING STOCK OF WHERE you fall on the need hierarchy will help you determine what kind of man you're most compatible with. A good match is most likely between two people who are close to the same need level. It's not necessary to be an exact match, but you want to be in the same ballpark. If one of you is much higher than the other, there's the danger that one person will bear the load of carrying the other, or alternately, pull the other one down. If you are self-actualized or nearing self-actualization, a man at a significantly lower level could cause you to slip down or regress.

Take a few minutes to complete the needs inventory below. Circle the statements that best fit you.

1. My physiological needs for nourishment, sex, and sleep are

   pretty much satisfied   *almost satisfied*   *not really satisfied*

2. My safety and security needs are

   pretty much satisfied   *almost satisfied*   *not really satisfied*

3. My needs for love and belonging are

   pretty much satisfied   *almost satisfied*   *not really satisfied*

4. My needs for self-respect and the respect of others are

   pretty much satisfied   *almost satisfied*   *not really satisfied*

5. My needs for things like creativity and peak experiences are

   pretty much satisfied   *almost satisfied*   *not really satisfied*

For questions 1–4, if your needs are almost satisfied or pretty much satisfied, you're probably about ready to move up to the next level on the need hierarchy. If you circled almost satisfied or pretty much satisfied for question 5, keep doing what you are doing, because it's fantastic that you are living your life creatively and enjoying peak experiences.

Your needs that are not really satisfied are going to be your current and future priorities. What need level are you most focused on now?

A Model Man for a Model Woman

THE PORTRAIT PRESENTED of Mr. Self-Actualized is a model of an amazing guy but not necessarily your idea of an amazing guy. As you read over Mr. Self-Actualized's top ten characteristics, some of you might not have thought they were so right for you; instead of humble, some of you might get turned on by cocky dudes, or maybe you prefer a guy with a raunchier sense of humor than Mr. Self-Actualized. The point is, start out with Mr. Self-Actualized's characteristics as a guideline and then tailor your profile of Mr. Right accordingly!

For those of you who thought that Mr. Self-Actualized is your ideal man, use the top ten characteristics as a mirror. If you want this guy—really, really want this guy—it's a must to bring out these qualities in yourself because that's what he'll be looking for in his Ms. Right.

Take a little time out for some honest self-examination and ask yourself some of these questions:

- Have I been nurturing my creative side enough lately?
- Am I letting my warmth show through, or have a few bad experiences made me too cold?
- Have I kept myself open to having peak experiences?
- Is my independence driven by my being my own woman, or does it come from fear of letting others in?
- Do I still have a sense of wonder about the world, or have I replaced it with boredom?
- If a certain ennui has crept into my life, what steps can I take to let the wonder back in?

Remember that one of the surest ways to prevent you from ever meeting Mr. Self-Actualized is to stay stuck in a stale relationship with Mr. Totally Unactualized. If you're currently dating someone who doesn't come close to having Mr. Self-Actualized's characteristics, it's a good time to examine what you expect out of this relationship.

Date with a Narcissist

"NARCISSIST," THE ELEGANT, technical word for thinking one is the center of the universe, is derived from the mythological character Narcissus. After seeing his own reflection in a shimmering pool of water, he fell in love with himself. The real tragedy of the story is poor Echo, the nymph who became infatuated with him only to be scorned. In an attempt to get away from her, Narcissus cried, "Hands off! Embrace me not! May I die before I give you power o'er me!"[1]

Clearly, Narcissus is not the type to give in to a female and resents anyone who tries to come between him and himself. When Echo finally sees that he is incapable of loving her, or anyone else, for that matter, she allows herself to be consumed by grief. In the end, Echo is reduced to a faint, reverberating voice that can only repeat the words of others.

The point of this chapter is to help you avoid poor Echo's fate because, as you can see, men who follow in Narcissus's footsteps have a long history of making women feel terrible. A woman's own insecurities may emerge when she thinks, "Well, he's not into me, so *I* must not be attractive or interesting enough for him." Wrong! No one could get through to Narcissus.

Unfortunately, more than a few women have encountered the untouchable narcissist. Have you ever had the uncontrollable urge to burst out singing Carly Simon's "You're So Vain" because of a man's obvious all-about-me attitude? This type of guy doesn't tax your profiling skills much—he's too easy to spot. There are, however, some narcissistic personalities that present more of a challenge to you, because recognizing the warning signs is a bit trickier.

Have you ever had the vague impression and unsatisfying sense that the man in your life doesn't fully listen to you? Is he so preoccupied with thoughts of his wonderful self or his own needs that you can't seem to get close—ever? If so, you may be having a run-in with Narcissus.

Characteristics of a Narcissist

THE THREE BASIC FEATURES of narcissistic personality disorder, as listed in the *Diagnostic and Statistical Manual of Mental Disorders*, are an inflated sense of self-importance, a need for constant admiration, and a lack of concern for the well-being of others.[2]

Without a doubt, when you get these three characteristics wrapped up in one man, you're in for a high-maintenance relationship! Just the act of continuously having to feed this inflated ego is enough to drain anyone's energy. Because of his general lack of empathy for others, there's no way he cares about what his neediness is doing to the woman in his life.

Ironically, underneath all the arrogance and conceit lies an itty-bitty, pea-sized ego that is highly vulnerable to being damaged.

Picture a giant red helium balloon as the inflated part of his ego. Inside the red balloon is a tiny green pea, which is the weak part of his ego. The only protection that wrinkled little pea has is a bunch of hot air and gas surrounding it. All it takes is a sharp comment or penetrating insight to burst that baby!

Looking at it this way, it's easier to understand why he keeps women at a distance. He sees them as a bunch of sharp objects ready to pierce him. He is afraid that a woman will see him for what he is and withdraw her love. Therefore, he keeps pumping himself up and putting others down, all the while trying to hide his insecurities.

More Narcissism

THE FOLLOWING DESCRIPTIONS SHOW in more detail what it's like to date Narcissus. Keep this short poem in mind as you read on:

> He—"Your eyes are so beautiful,
> upon close inspection;
> They're almost clear enough
> to see my reflection."

ME, MYSELF, AND I

Narcissus lets us know, "I burn with love of my own self."[3] He is hopelessly devoted to "me, myself, and I." Frequently, you notice him acting overly cocky, being boastful, and playing the conceited snob. His general attitude is that the world revolves around him and owes him something as well.

A date with a narcissist often seems like a monologue because he loves to do the talking. Jennifer, a thirty-four-year-old accountant, found this out the hard way on her date with Azul, a thirty-five-year-old sports commentator. Azul did ask Jennifer several perfunctory questions about herself, but it was nothing compared to the long commentary he provided about himself. Toward the end of the evening, Jennifer estimated that he had talked about 90 percent of the time compared to her 9 percent and the cheerful waiter's 1 percent.

Azul's self-absorption made Jennifer laugh when he said, "I've been asking you a lot of questions, but you haven't really asked me anything. Is there something you want to know about me?" By that point, Jennifer felt like she knew it all and then some!

If you find yourself in a similar situation, try playing a little game to alleviate the boredom. Count the number of times he says the words "I," "me," or "my" in five minutes. Later on, count the number of times a nonnarcissistic friend of yours says these words in the same period. Odds are you'll be shocked at how many more times the narcissist refers to himself.

If you have been or are currently dating someone who fits this description, you've probably learned that fights, debates, or discussions with him can be infuriating. Because he fancies himself as the center of the universe, he is also the center of truth and light. For Narcissus, objective reality, scientific truths, research studies, and informed opinions don't mean much.

If you point to the sky and say, "It's blue," he would have no problem saying, "You're wrong, the sky is green." The fact that he believes the sky to be green automatically transforms it into a universal truth. Sticking to your guns on this argument will only make it worse; he'll argue with you until the last dog dies.

Whenever you contradict Narcissus's opinions or beliefs, in his eyes you are launching a personal attack. His shriveled-up, pea-sized ego becomes more vulnerable when he perceives you calling him "wrong." He takes any disagreements you have with him very personally and may launch a vicious counterattack to deflect what he views as harsh criticism.

MIRROR, MIRROR ON THE WALL

In preparation for her college formal, Jessica had spent the better part of the afternoon primping, fluffing, and spraying. She couldn't wait to see Brad's expression when he came to pick her up and saw the beautiful dress she was wearing. It wasn't her normal routine to spend a lot of time on her appearance, but this day was special and she thought Brad was special.

As Jessica opened the door, she locked eyes with him in order to get the full impact of his reaction. Instead of pausing, as she thought he would, Brad smiled and brushed past her.

Once inside, he did a little dance step and turned toward her. The first words out of Brad's mouth to Jessica were, "Do I look good, or do I look gooood?!" At the last syllable of "gooood," he rhythmically crossed the room to take a look in the mirror. About twenty minutes later, Brad managed to tell Jessica that she looked pretty too, but it was definitely a case of too little too late.

Brad's excessive display of vanity is one of the most blatant manifestations of narcissism. A guy who is overly caught up in his coif, his muscles, his tan, or anything else about himself you can think of should give you pause. Remember, if he's always looking at himself, how could he have the time to look at you?

If, however, you come across a guy who takes pride in his appearance and puts some effort into it, don't overreact and start hiding the mirrors. Most likely, he's an average guy trying to make an impression on you. Moreover, it's important to note that not every narcissistic man focuses on his looks. His self-centeredness can come out in other ways—some of which are easy to recognize and some of which are more difficult to spot.

TROPHY DATING AND FLATTERY

When he wants to be, Narcissus can be quite good at flattery. Perhaps because he constantly seeks out flattery, he's practiced at giving good flattery. At times, his compliments may seem overdone and obsequious, but often the sweet talk can feel genuine. In fact, it may be genuine, but the problem is that genuine for Narcissus and genuine for a man who is not narcissistic are two totally different things.

Remember, Narcissus is *always* out to puff up his own ego, which he does in either one of two ways. Number one, he criticizes other people so that he looks better by comparison. Number two, he attempts to associate himself with people whom he deems special so that some of their specialness will rub off on him. In other words, his self-esteem gets a boost when he sees the qualities he wants to possess "mirrored" in the people he hangs out with.[4] And he's very willing to use flattery to get these special people close to him.

This need to look good by association is why narcissists are particularly prone to trophy dating. They often want a women with looks, intelligence, and personality on their arm—the key phrase being "on their arm." Rather than seeing a woman as a unique and special person in her own right, the narcissistic man sees her as an ornament. He wants an object with which to adorn himself. Deep down inside, narcissistic men feel like the emperor with no clothes, so they go to great lengths not to have their tiny, naked egos exposed. Trophy dating is one way to cover up.

Of course, as soon as the ornament starts to outshine him, the worm can turn awfully quickly. Flattery can twist into subtle insults in the blink of an eye. If Narcissus feels that the woman on his arm is outshining rather than enhancing him, she's history.

PATHOLOGICAL ENVY

Envy plays a major part in the narcissistic personality. A narcissist tends to envy other people or think that everybody envies him.[5] Of course, envy is a natural human feeling that all of us share. The difference is that everyday envy doesn't infect the average person to the degree that it does the narcissist.

A man who suffers from pathological envy is liable to resent the times that you outshine him and begrudge your successes. The following are a few of the many things that may trigger his envy:

- getting more attention at a party than he does
- knowing a fact that he doesn't know
- having success at your job
- being in a better mood than he is that day

What effect does his envy have on you? First, you notice that you're getting dragged into a lot of one-upmanship games like, "If you think your day was bad, just listen to my day!" or "Anything you can do, I can do better." And of course there's everybody's favorite, "Mine's bigger than yours!"

Second, you begin to feel that he is diminishing you as a person. Because he seeks superiority, he must find ways to put you down. He must find ways to punish you when he feels envy overtaking him. It might begin subtly at first with a backhanded compliment here or there. Soon, however, it becomes all too easy to notice the pattern of put-downs designed to puff up his own deflating ego.

"IT'S NEWS TO ME"

Interestingly, the narcissistic man may, at times, appear ditsy or clueless. Because he doesn't care about what anyone else is saying, he doesn't listen well and the information doesn't get internalized. It's like the conversation never gets fully processed. Everything anyone tells him becomes so forgettable that it's all news to him.

Start hoisting the red flag if after repeating yourself over and over he says things like:

- I had no idea you felt that way.
- Well, that's the first time I've heard about it.
- Say what?
- You could have told me.
- No way?!

Once again, it is important not to jump to conclusions. Just because he overlooks Valentine's Day or forgets what you're saying to him during the NCAA playoffs doesn't mean he's Narcissus reincarnated. You might be dating the absentminded professor type whose forgetfulness is equal opportunity and not self-centered (this absentmindedness can actually be an endearing quality to some). The narcissistic version is forgetfulness directed at you, a constant, general sense of, "Huh, what'd you say?"

INSENSITIVE TO THE BONE

Because the narcissistic man is always thinking about himself, he can never really gauge what other people are thinking or feeling. It's not uncommon for this type of guy to make hurtful or insulting comments without even knowing it.

Take Arianna's first and last date at a trendy bistro with Michael, a thirty-eight-year-old pediatrician. As they were being seated, Arianna commented on how much she liked the strolling guitar player's music. Before she finished her sentence, Michael, in a really, really loud voice, declared, "In about five minutes, you'll be wanting to pay the dude to get away from the table with his damn guitar."

Every single person around them, including the waiter and the dude with the guitar, heard his uncalled-for comment and shot nasty looks at their table. While Michael remained oblivious to the entire situation, Arianna spent the rest of the night being overly nice to the restaurant staff to compensate for his bad behavior.

It's important to note that if narcissistic Michael had actually noticed the hubbub he caused, he might have felt sorry—but not sorry for hurting the musician's feelings, sorry because he embarrassed himself. This is a significant difference, because sometimes a narcissist might seem remorseful about something he has said to hurt you when he's really just sorry for himself.

The narcissistic man's insensitivity can have two aspects: He's generally unable to get a good read on you and the people around him, and, if he is able to interpret a situation accurately, as long as it doesn't affect him, "Who cares?"

IN LOVE WITH LOVE

At first glance, the guy who is in love with love can seem like a real catch. He may create an atmosphere of romance for you that's similar to a scene out of your favorite romantic movie—rose petals, wine, and candles. He may say dreamy things like how your beauty is overwhelming and how he has never felt this way before. The problem is if it's Narcissus, more likely than not he has felt this way a dozen times before.

How can someone experience such powerful feelings of love over and over again? Unfortunately, the answer is all too simple: A guy who is in love with being in love can never love a *specific* woman. For him, women are interchangeable. Each female is nothing more than a mirror for his narcissistic fantasies. Again, it's all about him.

When a therapist is considering diagnosing someone with narcissistic personality disorder, one of the things he or she looks for is an obsession with ideal love and never-ending success.[6] While many people have daydreams of the perfect love and success, the difference is that all the narcissistic man sees are his own unrealistic internal desires and dreams. The narcissistic man never, ever really sees you.

Not only doesn't he ever really see you, according to research, he's also going to be reluctant to commit to you. Love and commitment don't necessarily go together for Narcissus. In fact, narcissism is actually negatively related to commitment, mainly because this guy is always looking for the next best thing to come along.[7]

A Matter of Degree

WHEN TAKING ALL the characteristics of Narcissus into account, it's important to put them into perspective. Don't become too concerned if a man is simply trying to impress you with his accomplishments. Men often attempt to project an air of confidence that can verge on cocky while dating.

Additionally, most people probably have tendencies toward many of the traits described in this chapter. After all, who doesn't have a vain or selfish moment? The problem is when a moment becomes eternal: That's the shift from semi-self-absorbed to meganarcissist.

Dating Narcissus is an emotionally lonely and draining enterprise. Worse yet, the prognosis for him to make a major change for the better is slim to none. Unless he manages a bit of insight (perhaps some kind of life-altering experience that takes his falsely inflated ego down a peg or two), he will remain as he is.

A relationship with him will be filled with chilliness, envy, and indifference. The best strategy in this case is *not* to stick around like poor Echo did. Narcissus sucked the soul out of her so hard and so fast that in the end she lost her true voice.

9

Passion, Power, and Paranoia

THE LOVE STORY between Napoleon and Josephine is one of the most romantic and engaging in history. By most accounts, it was he who had the burden of being the partner more in love, while she took some pleasure in his overwhelming passion.[1] Wouldn't it be interesting to be worshipped by an emperor? Many women, probably more often than they would like to admit, daydream about eliciting this kind of passion in a man.

There is some thrill in knowing that your qualities can throw a particular man into a frenzy. A secret wish in the back of many of our minds might be to find a man who is devoted to us beyond reason. Unfortunately, as the saying goes, sometimes you have to be careful what you wish for. The fantasy may not always coordinate with the reality of what you need.

Indeed, Napoleon's love for Josephine wasn't all it's cracked up to be. Contemporaries of the couple who had read the famous love letters he wrote to her said Napoleon's words were "characterized by the utmost violence of passion," as well as showed "symptoms of jealousy, sometimes somber, sometimes menacing."[2] These descriptions don't exactly connote a warm and fuzzy kind of love, do they?

When someone loves that violently, he may be seeking power over the object of his affection. One way Napoleon exercised his power was to re-create Josephine's image to suit him. Not only did he assign her titles, but he also gave her a new name; she was actually called Rose until he changed it to Josephine.[3] Napoleon took it upon himself to mold her persona into *his* image of what an empress should be.

This chapter will help you identify the type of man who sees you as a country to conquer—who wants to take you over. While at first you may be swept away by his overwhelming passion for you, all too soon you may be left feeling alone and lost at sea. Power-hungry guys tend to structure relationships so that they are a woman's only life preserver. They seek control over women. Some may desire purely mental control; others may try to gain power through physical aggression.

The Paranoid Personality

THE PARANOID personality type has gotten tremendous attention in the psychology literature. The first image that comes to mind for many when they hear the word "paranoid" is some weasely guy sitting in a murky room thinking that the CIA together with alien life-forms are out to get him.

When people think of paranoia, they often associate it with an over-the-top degree of suspiciousness. In truth, there are individuals who have that extreme kind of paranoia. Chances are, however, if you run into a guy harping on conspiracies and people who are out to get him, you're not going to consider him prime date material.

But there are guys who have tendencies toward paranoia that are not evident immediately. For example, a man might read hidden meanings into your neutral comments. He might believe that you're lying to him when you're not or that you don't trust him when you do. It's also likely that he may become crazy-jealous for no good reason.

Clearly, there is a definite, underlying suspicion in someone who has paranoid tendencies, yet the concept of paranoia encompasses more than that. An equally important component is grandiosity.

Grandiosity causes the need for control. If the guy feels that everyone around him is out to attack, he seeks power and control to ward off the attack. A paranoid's prime motivation is being the king, with you and others as his subjects. A paranoid guy is a grandiose megalomaniac.

Sometimes the paranoid man is able to grab the kind of power he yearns for. History is littered with dictators, corporate giants, warriors, and world leaders who have been considered to have paranoid tendencies.

One of the first who comes to mind is Richard Nixon. He felt so watched by the Democratic Party that he was compelled to spy on them, causing the now famous Watergate scandal. Nixon's mistrust of everyone, preoccupation with his perceived enemies, and hostile us-versus-them attitude indicate he may have been paranoid.[4]

Dating Paranoid Guy

THE PROBLEM FOR WOMEN in terms of dating is that, at first glance, Paranoid Guy might appear to be a really attractive option. He can be bright, good-looking, and competent. If you meet him in college, he might be the president of his fraternity and seem like a guy who is going places. If you catch him in his thirties, he might be a rising star on Wall Street, in the film industry, or in politics. If you catch him in his fifties, he might be running a small business, be a corporate vice president, or be a vice presidential candidate. There are some telltale behaviors and characteristics that can give the paranoid guy away.

CHARISMA

Some paranoid guys let their suspicions drive them into isolation. They tend to keep to themselves and seem cold, defensive, and angry. Because of his isolationist tendencies, you're not as likely to encounter this paranoid guy.

The one to really watch out for is the charismatic paranoid. He may appear larger than life, as if he has the world at his fingertips and everyone at his command. He walks into a crowded room and people take notice. Boy, does he know how to work a room! Somehow he's temporarily able to hide all his suspicion and replace it with magnetism. Stalin, a consummate paranoid, was famous for his "charm and affability."[5]

The difference between Paranoid Guy and a nice, charismatic guy is that Paranoid Guy uses his skills to lure you in until he thinks he has you in his control and then he attempts to keep you with his power. The shift in his behavior can be startling. One minute he's all charm and the next he's trying to control your every move.

JEALOUSY AND MISTRUST

Paranoia can make a guy jealous of your interactions with other men even when there is no just cause for it. Occasionally, the fact that your man gets a little bit annoyed at a waiter flirting with you or an ex-boyfriend calling you may seem flattering. Somehow a moderate amount of jealousy can make a woman feel that a man is really interested. Some women admit to the coquette in them taking over to the point where they actually try to provoke jealousy in a man.

With Paranoid Guy, no provocation is necessary, and his level of jealousy is definitely not moderate. He confronts and accuses you about things that seem ludicrous to you. Repeated denials of infidelity don't convince him. There is always a part of him that thinks you and everyone else in the world are disloyal and can't be trusted.[6]

One way for him to keep his jealousy and mistrust in check is to limit your contacts with other men and the outside world in general. Paranoid Guy wants to be your world, so he systematically attempts to keep you away from interlopers. This means keeping you away not only from other men, but from everybody. You notice that he tries to whittle down girls' nights out, family time, and your personal time. He may call you frequently to check up on you, as well as make you account for your whereabouts.

The danger in this is losing your support system. Family and friends not only provide support but also serve to give you perspective on your personal life and dating. Paranoid Guy doesn't want family or friends telling you he's not what he wants you to believe.

Also, by limiting your personal time, he is taking away your ability to self-reflect. By keeping you overly occupied, even in sometimes fun ways, he limits your capacity for introspection. By doing this he is attempting to substitute his opinions and attitudes for your own. Paranoid Guy is jealous—jealous of other men, jealous of your relationships with friends and family, and perhaps worst of all, jealous of your independence of mind!

A MAD RUSH TO COMMIT

Paranoid Guy, in many cases, appears to be totally all about you. He may notice specific things about your personality that floor you. He may ask you pertinent, thoughtful questions and listen attentively to the answers. He may appear to be completely captivated by you. He probably does feel captivated . . . and now he wants to capture you.

Bear in mind that it's not easy for Paranoid Guy to be walking around with all this anger and mistrust. He wants so badly to find loyalty and love in a person that it can take on questlike proportions.[7] In the beginning, you're like a blank slate; he may not fully trust you, but you haven't "betrayed" him yet either.

Put yourself in his position for a minute. You've just met someone who you believe can turn your hostile, mistrustful feelings into loving feelings. What do you do? Well, you go after it full throttle. This guy is going to be in a mad, passionate rush to have you.

One of the best ways to distinguish between an average guy who likes you in a healthy way and Paranoid Guy is the mad rush. With Paranoid Guy you get the sense that your relationship is on fast-forward. Initially, for twenty-four-year-old Shelby, it seemed cool that Josh didn't want to see other women after only their second date. She was also fine with his preference that she not see other men.

In Shelby's mind, Josh's eagerness to be exclusive was a sign that he really liked her and was commitment-ready. Unfortunately, it turned out to be the first in a series of signs that indicated his paranoid tendencies. Right away, he made the assumption that they should spend Friday and Saturday nights "as a couple." When Shelby didn't abide by this rule on their fourth weekend together, she had a vague sense of his unexpressed anger.

By week five, his jealousy regarding her platonic male friends and coworkers started to leak out, which had the effect of making Shelby ever so slightly pull away from him. Like a bloodhound sniffing out its quarry, Josh detected her subtle effort to distance herself and pounced. He wrote Shelby a long e-mail detailing his concern about her fear of intimacy and her coldness.

At first, Shelby gave the e-mail some credence. Maybe she was cold and walled off. What if Josh was right? After all, he gave her so much attention, why wouldn't she want to give an equal amount back? For a while, she really tried. The problem was that no matter how much she gave, it was never enough. It became a drain on her energy to have to prove her feelings for Josh hour after hour, minute after minute.

When she finally decided that it wasn't her intimacy issues but his control issues that were dooming the relationship, Shelby decided to get out with one swift, quick stroke. Although her friends told her it seemed hard-hearted, she broke up with him over the phone to avoid an aggressive confrontation. As you probably guessed, Josh didn't let her go easily. There were angry phone calls, several more e-mails, a couple of "accidental" meetings at places where he knew she hung out, and other attempts to prove she was wrong to end things.

In this case, however, Josh's postbreakup power trip did taper off. A combination of Shelby's unwavering response to his pleas and her good sense in stopping the relationship in its semi-early stages helped to prevent a more unfortunate end to this story.

Still, there is something tragic about the doomed aspect of a paranoid man's search for love. He's always mired in a Catch-22. He needs love as a bandage for the hurt of his inner mistrustfulness, but once he gets love he can never really trust it. Instead, he tries to gain control over it, which can't get him what he needs.

Incidentally, sometimes your own needs can get in the way of profiling this guy soon enough. If you are in a vulnerable state due to a recent breakup, a dip in your self-esteem, or just suffering from general loneliness, you can fall prey to the mad rush. The problem is that unhealthy relationships are often easier to fall into than to get out of; hence the importance of taking the yellow light approach when faced with the mad rush.

A BLACK-AND-WHITE WORLDVIEW

For Paranoid Guy, shades of gray don't exist. He needs to see things as black or white because the ambiguity of gray makes him feel out of control. In his views on current affairs and politics, you might notice an us-versus-them mentality. The people placed in the "them" category are often dangerously vilified. There is good and bad, loyal and disloyal, angel and whore.

At the beginning of your dating experience with Paranoid Guy, it's likely that he puts you in the good, loyal, angel group. He's awesome at treating his angel like an angel. The bad news is that if you get kicked over to the whore side, watch out for the nurturing to disappear and the cruelty and control to begin!

A woman can be labeled a whore for anything—questioning his opinions, smiling at a store clerk, not having dinner ready on time—anything he sees as a form of betrayal. Some women get caught in the trap of trying to anticipate what will set him off and expend an enormous amount of energy trying to keep the peace. Doing so is a waste of time and won't last. He's best left alone—the sooner the better.

In his black-and-white world, everything has its place. And he is the one who controls everything's place. Paranoid Guy may appear orderly, self-disciplined, and efficient, but scratch the surface and you get rigidity, dogmatism, and inflexibility. He is on a mission to stomp out chaos.

On a date, any guy with a black-and-white attitude is pretty easy to cull out. Even if he keeps it undercover, with awareness you'll see the behavior. If you feel inflexibility might be staring you in the face, ask yourself:

- Does he frequently stereotype?
- Does he overgeneralize? For example, instead of saying,

"That woman is judgmental," does he say, "All women are judgmental"?

- Is he always focusing on the rules without noting the exceptions to the rules?
- Does he use words like "always," "never," and "absolutely" instead of words like "perhaps," "maybe," or "sometimes"?

Take some time to think about guys you've dated. In what ways did they show a black-and-white attitude? Just as important, in what ways are you black and white? Are there things about which you think you should be more flexible?

PARANOID . . . NOT!

Another good way to profile for the paranoid, controlling type of guy is to compare his behavior with positive personality traits, like the following:[8]

Not Paranoid and Controlling	Paranoid and Controlling
introspective	always looking outside himself
modest	self-righteous and arrogant
candid	evasive
acknowledges his own flaws	acknowledges everyone else's flaws

READING BETWEEN THE LINES

Everyone has tendencies to read into the things people say. The truth isn't always contained in the words people speak; it can be lurking somewhere below the surface. Have you ever accepted praise from a coworker, only to realize a second later that it was a back-handed compliment? Maybe you've read a little white lie into a statement your boyfriend wanted you to accept as the truth?

The difference between the Paranoid Guy and everyone else is that reading between the lines is a way of life for him, and he's constantly finding hidden meanings where there are none. In every word and gesture, our paranoid friend is looking for a lie, a put-down, a secret not revealed, or some surreptitious agenda.

Kim, a dental hygienist, found out what it feels like to be the recipient of paranoid mistrustfulness starting around the fifth date with a forty-year-old dentist named Jim. Initially, he was so interested in her that she was thinking, "Maybe this is the one!" But then, incident by incident, Kim started to wonder. One day, Jim overheard a phone conversation between Kim and her mother that made him suspicious. Kim was sharing the details of a fun dinner party Jim had taken her to the night before.

A couple of hours later, out of the blue, Kim found herself confronted by Jim asking, "Why did you lie to your mother?" Confounded, all she could reply was, "What are you talking about?" Apparently, Jim had been brooding over the belief that Kim didn't have a good time at the party although she said she did.

Kim had enjoyed herself very much but for the life of her could not convince Jim that she wasn't lying. Almost immediately, she began looking inward, trying to figure out what *she* was doing to cause Jim's doubtfulness. As Jim's doubtfulness grew in their relationship, so did Kim's self-blame.

More and more often, he began to accuse her of doing things like leaving her coat on the chair to "purposely annoy" him. She thought she was just being lazy about putting her coat away, but then she reconsidered, wondering if it could have been subconsciously purposeful. There were times when a laugh on her part would be mistaken for mockery by Jim.

For a while, walking on eggshells was a way of life for Kim so as not to make Jim angry. What finally gave Kim some clarity on the matter was his almost violent reaction to an insignificant incident at an outdoor festival. A man walked past Jim, grazed his shoulder, and spilled about a tablespoon of beer on him. The man apologized profusely, but that didn't stop Jim's face from turning to stone. Kim felt like if she didn't get him away from the guy, Jim was going to beat him to the ground.

Kim finally saw it: Just as this man had done nothing to provoke Jim, she hadn't been doing anything to provoke Jim either. He was the one falsely speed-reading between the lines. Everything was in *his* head! It also made her nervous that he seemed ready to respond to a minor confrontation with violence so quickly. Would she be the recipient of this type of aggression later in the relationship? Quicker than she could answer this question to herself, she decided to break up with Jim . . . in a very public place.

Vicious and Violent

THE PARANOID MAN is just one type who may want to grab control over you. There are others. For some men, taking control means physically beating a woman into submission. There may be a tendency to think that married women are more likely to be abused than single women; however, as it turns out, single, divorced, and separated women are at a greater risk for battering.[9] Taking control by profiling dates can weed out the potentially dangerous guy early on.

Eve S. Buzawa and Carl G. Buzawa reviewed many studies in this area and identified several "risk markers for batterers" that can help you spot a propensity for intimate violence:[10]

LOW SELF-ESTEEM. He feels down on himself and powerless, so he retaliates by physically attacking a woman.

ANGER MANAGEMENT PROBLEMS. He's an angry, hostile, generally negative guy who flies off the handle and doesn't choose to control himself. Rather, he chooses to control a woman through violence and intimidation.

IMMATURE. Like a child, the guy tries to minimize the harm he causes while at the same time shifting blame to the woman: "She provoked me; it's her fault."

ABUSES DRUGS AND/OR ALCOHOL. It's likely he is a substance abuser as well as a woman abuser. One study showed that at the time of their violent outbursts, 70 percent of the batterers were under the influence of drugs, alcohol, or both.

EXPERIENCES OF CHILDHOOD VIOLENCE. He probably had a bad childhood. Frequently, the batterer has learned to make an association between love and violence due to an aggressive and violent upbringing. It may be that he was a target of violence and/or a witness of violent acts, such as looking on as his father hit his mother.

POOR CONFLICT RESOLUTION SKILLS. He misperceives a woman's attempt to communicate with him as an attack and is also unable to adequately express his own feelings, particularly anger. Expressing other emotions, such as sadness or anxiety, poses a problem for him because he may perceive these expressions as displays of vulnerability.

A WIDE RANGE OF MENTAL ILLNESSES. He probably has some psychological issues. Research has shown that batterers are thirteen times more likely to have some form of mental illness, including depression, schizophrenia, antisocial personality disorder (sociopathy), and even anxiety disorders.

HIGH TESTOSTERONE LEVELS. He may have a higher level of testosterone than the norm. Men with higher testosterone levels have been shown to be more violent than those with lower levels.

A GENERALLY VIOLENT BEING. More likely than not, he has been violent with other people, including men and women.

These risk markers for a battering man paint a clear picture of what you need to avoid. If the man you've been seeing has a few of these ingredients, be extremely leery of what you're getting yourself into, because once the cycle of violence has started, it is incredibly hard to stop.

There are three phases to the cycle of violence:[12]

* tension building
* emotional/physical abuse
* remorse

In the tension-building phase, it is as though you can sense a storm coming. There is a heavy feeling of dread and inevitability. For example, he might be touchy, resentful, and easily irritated.

In the second phase, the storm arrives in the form of emotional and physical abuse. Earlier in the relationship, the beating and be-littling may be less severe—a push, a slap, one punch, or some de-grading name-calling. As the cycle spins forward, it usually escalates, sometimes with deadly results.

The remorse phase adds complexity to the cycle of violence and gives the rotation much of its impetus. After the blowup and abuse, many batterers show remorse. Some may feel genuine remorse, but many display phony remorse. Either way, a man's remorse has no credence unless he stops the abusive behavior.

To win their partners over, batterers try to make it up to them during this remorse phase. If a woman was abused without a break in this passionate, honeymoonlike period, it would be much easier for her to get out.

With all the I'm-sorry-I-promise-it-will-never-happen-again speeches accompanied by kisses and gifts, some women tend to give batterers another chance . . . and another . . . and another. Particu-larly if the abuse is seemingly minor, women may minimize vio-lence as "only a slap" that he didn't mean or, worse yet, blame themselves for eliciting the abuse. Because it's easy to get trapped, avoiding the cycle of violence instead of getting caught up in it is so important!

Spotting a Potential Stalker

STALKING IS NOT INDICATIVE OF true passion; it's about power . . . and loss of power. The stalker you've had a relationship with feels as if his life will career out of control once you're gone, so the only thing to do is to get you back. Orit Kamir, author of *Every Breath You Take*, puts it this way: "Stalking is a response to feeling left out in the past by the other person. It is the stalker's struggle to move (back) into the other person's life, which the stalker perceives as the inside, the present, the center of everything that is meaningful."[12]

To get back to that center, the stalker uses controlling behaviors that impinge on your freedom. He may hound you through phone calls, letters, e-mails, and gift giving. He may follow you, harass your friends and family, or threaten you. He may carry out his threats.

One of the biggest fears women have about dating is coming across a potential stalker. The best thing you can do with this type of guy is nip the relationship in the bud and end contact with a swift, clean break. Following are some questions to ask yourself and/or him (in a subtle way) on a date to help you spot a potential stalker.

HOW DOES HE CHARACTERIZE HIS PAST RELATIONSHIPS?

A great thing to find out is if he has ever initiated breakups; stalkers are seldom the ones to end a relationship.[13] Also, does he blame his exes for everything without assuming any responsibility himself? Does he seem disproportionately bitter and hurt, without being able to let go? If so, even if the guy's not a stalker, you might want to reconsider going out on another date.

DOES HE OBSESS?

Try to assess if he tends to fixate on people or issues, particularly but not limited to things related to women and relationships.

- Does he fixate on the faithfulness of the woman he's seeing?
- Is he seized by panic about the future of a relationship after the first date?

- Do minor on-the-job problems consume him?
- Is he preoccupied with issues from his past?

WHAT DOES HE *REALLY* THINK OF WOMEN?

Try to find out if he admires and respects women who are intelligent and independent. Stalkers are typically threatened by these qualities. Look for negative attitudes toward women that he might display through degrading comments or behaviors.

IS HE YOUNGER THAN FORTY?

Younger men are more likely than older ones to stalk and commit violent acts.[14]

IS HE DOWN ON HIMSELF?

Stalkers tend to have low self-esteem.[15] They feel bad and empty inside and are in desperate need of someone like you to validate their existence. Keep in mind that low self-esteem, which can be evidenced through self-deprecating comments, may present itself in the opposite way: through excessive bragging and conceit. Take note of a man who seems very unsure of himself, or a guy who goes overboard trying to impress you with his qualities.

DOES HE HAVE A FULL LIFE AND A GOOD SUPPORT SYSTEM?

If a man's got a busy schedule that he enjoys, he's probably not going to have time to stalk you. Someone who is into his career, pursues activities such as music or sports for pleasure and, in general, finds

creative ways to occupy his time is a safer bet for a date than someone who has less going on in his life. Having a strong network of
friends and family is also a good sign. If you break up with him, then
he'll have other people to turn to for emotional support.

You will get a clue to his connection with friends and family though
his casual conversation, such as, "I spent all day Saturday at a family
barbeque" or "I'm going to my old high school friend's wedding."
Also, as you see him more, you should be introduced to the important
people in his life on double dates, at parties, and at other events.

IS HE PUSHY?

Something is awry if a man wants too much from you too soon. You
should never feel pushed or rushed into emotional or sexual intimacy. A danger point here is that the push can serve to flatter your
vanity. It's so much nicer to think, "Oh, he's rushing because he's so
in love with me," versus, "He is pushing because he's a creepy guy
with serious issues!"

Too many phone calls, too many dates, too many presents in the
beginning of a relationship are a red flag. If too much is happening
too soon, you probably also notice that he has problems with the
word "no." Does he frequently persist in steering you away from a no
answer until you relent with a yes? Does he often coax and cajole you
to get his way?

On your next date, the "Is he pushy?" question may prove to have
a clear-cut answer: "Yes, he's a freaky, pushy jerk!" or "No, he hasn't
been controlling tonight at all." Sometimes, however, you may find
that you have difficulty distinguishing between pushiness and perseverance.

In this culture, it's not only socially acceptable but also socially
desirable for a man to be an aggressive go-getter. Many women find

being able to set goals and having the determination to achieve them attractive qualities in a man. Recent cultural phenomena such as *The Apprentice* glorify this quality in business. When a man has his eye on the prize, especially when the prize is you, he should persist, should he not? Well, if it's a Hollywood movie you're watching, the answer is probably yes. If it's real life, not necessarily.

Think about how many movies you've seen in which the heroine flat-out rejects the hero, but he pursues her anyway. Ultimately he wins her love. It's not at all unusual for the line between courtship persistence and stalking to become extremely blurred in films.[16]

Often what seems crazy-romantic in movies seems just plain crazy when it happens in real life. When you flat-out reject a guy in real life, he needs to stop the chase. If you've given a clear "No!" and he doesn't hear it, something's wrong. Perseverance itself isn't bad. It just needs to be welcomed by you. Once you've given the green light, let the chase begin!

Proceed with Caution, Not Fear

WHILE IT'S ESSENTIAL to become aware of the possible paranoia and power plays behind certain men's passion, it shouldn't make you fearful of dating. Having a man who has a healthy excitement and passion about you is wonderful and something to revel in. The key is making the distinction between healthy passion and violent passion.

A commonality among controlling types of men, including para-noids, batterers, and stalkers, is that they tend to encroach on your freedom from the beginning. If you're dating one, you might get the sense that a person who was a stranger to you a short while ago is now enmeshed in your life. You might find yourself wondering, "How did this man get so fast and so deep into my existence?"

Any man who has good and true passion for you does not invade your life; he enhances it. Pleasure for him comes from watching you flourish freely. He makes it his business to open up the world for you and help you to see all the choices that lie ahead. This is quite different from a man who hides your choices from you, draws boundaries, places restrictions, and boxes you in.

The Everyday Sociopath and Lie Detecting

ALL OF US HAVE SEEN the überviolent serial-killer sociopath sensationalized in the media and entertainment industry. Think of the fictitious Hannibal Lecter or the all-too-real Ted Bundy/Boston Strangler types. Obviously, they are the extremes in sociopathic thought and behavior.

Fortunately you're unlikely to run into this extreme, but you do need to keep an eye out for the lower-grade "everyday" sociopath.[1] He is potentially more dangerous because the probability of running into him is higher.

He is the guy who has the ability to charm a woman's pants off . . . maybe literally. He may not necessarily be as dangerous as a serial killer, yet he may prove to be a dire threat in terms of your psychological well-being and/or a danger to you physically.

He might not be a full-blown sociopath but have a few sociopathic tendencies roaming around in his psyche. "Tendencies" can seem minor, but in a relationship they loom very large.

His manipulation and deceit, his thrill-seeking behaviors, as well as his lack of empathy can be jarring. Don't let yourself be taken in by the everyday sociopath. Through profiling, you can learn how to cut through his charm, pierce his lies, and duck his manipulation.

Cold Thoughts and Cold Words

IN KEVIN COSTNER'S 2003 testosterone-fueled western, *Open Range*, his tough and wise cowboy character, Charley, advises, "Most time[s] a man will tell you his bad intentions if you listen—let yourself hear."

The following statements reveal the hard-hearted attitude of the everyday sociopath in terms of relationships and general worldview. It may take time for him to verbalize his cold worldview this blatantly, but if you let yourself hear, you'll be able to catch glimpses of it in both words and actions.

- You always gotta look out for number one.
- She was good for about six months. I'm done now, though . . . I got what I wanted.
- In all situations, you need to ask yourself, "What am I gonna get out of it?"
- All those b*#@*s got what they deserved from me.
- I need the kind of girl who can hold my attention and rein me in.
- I don't need people to keep lecturing me about what's right and wrong. I'm the one who defines what's right and wrong.

The Everyday Sociopath's Behavior

AN EVERYDAY SOCIOPATH truly has no regard for anyone but himself. It makes him a pretty lousy boyfriend. Let's take a more detailed look at the behavior of the everyday sociopath and whet he's like in a relationship.

HE'S ALWAYS BORED

An everyday sociopath has a propensity for being bored. Life's simple pleasures, like going out to eat, watching a good movie, or spending laid-back time with friends and family, just don't do it for him. Unless it's a night of drinking, gambling, chasing after women, or other general carousing/thrill-seeking behavior, the everyday sociopath probably feels like it's a wasted evening.

Does this mean that you have to watch out for every guy who likes to party or seek some thrills once in a while? No. You want to home in on the ones who are pattern partiers and seem unable to enjoy calmer, everyday pursuits.

Twenty-eight-year-old Kenna noticed that her boyfriend Blake's word for just about everything was "tame." If he wasn't drunk or risking his neck at some extreme sport, whatever he did that week, that day, that hour was "tame." Slowly but surely, Kenna began to realize that her new-girlfriend glow was dimming and that she was fast becoming lumped in with all that was "tame."

Unfortunately, she took on the responsibility for trying to alleviate his perpetual boredom. She actually got upset with herself for being "just a girl." "How could 'just a girl' keep a man like this?" she thought.

The burden of entertaining Blake weighed heavily on her, but Kenna tried. She tried to plan things to do that he might like. She tried to be witty and funny and upbeat. She tried so hard that he noticed and took a kind of sick pleasure in showing that he was more bored than ever.

Then came the ironic twist. Kenna got bored! At first, she was intrigued by what seemed to be an interesting bad boy. But the fact was that Blake was the one who was boring. He didn't have the ability to make day-to-day life interesting. Suddenly, being "just a girl" didn't seem so horrible to Kenna after all. At least she was a girl who had the capacity to make life interesting for herself.

In general, Blake and other sociopaths tend to have a very high threshold for stimulation, meaning that it takes an awful lot to excite them. They also have poor impulse control, so when they see something that will excite them for the moment, they're liable to act on it despite the consequences.

In a relationship, this constant need for instant gratification and stimulation can be a real problem. Even if he seems to have settled down for a while, that itch for excitement may need to be scratched at any moment. If there is no excitement around, he tries to create his own negative drama. "Callous and predatory acts, flagrant violation of social norms, and outrageous deceits are all diversions that help them create a sense of excitement that saturates the moment with sensation."[2] When sociopaths get bored with their girlfriends, physical and/or psychological abuse may be a quick fix of stimulation for them.

In an attempt to study sociopaths/psychopaths—the ones who aren't in prison or the mental-heath system—a researcher placed the following ad to get recruits:

Psychologist studying adventurous carefree people who've led exciting, impulsive lives. If you're the kind of person who'd do almost anything for a dare and want to participate in a paid experiment, send name, address, phone, and short biography proving how interesting you are to . . . [3]

Take note of the descriptors, including "adventurous," "carefree," and "exciting." This researcher cleverly used words that don't have particularly negative connotations. In general, a sociopath isn't going to identify himself to you by saying he's irresponsible, reckless, or careless.

Instead, he may let the cat out of the bag with self-descriptors like risk taking, daring, living for the moment, and perhaps even courageous. First and foremost, watch out for any guy who refers to himself in this way. If you go on the Internet, you'll be surprised by how many personality profiles resemble the ad this researcher used to recruit sociopaths. So unless you're trying to recruit one as a boyfriend, beware of the self-described "impulsive, carefree adventurer."

Of course, not every risk-taking, adventurous type is a sociopath. Many men who have achieved remarkable accomplishments have managed to channel their adventurous spirit in socially acceptable and even admirable ways. They also may be quite ethical with regard to how they carry out their adventures. That's a key distinction between a rugged risk taker and an everyday sociopath. The sociopath is not concerned with right and wrong, only about what's right for him.

For instance, although Robin Hood was basically an adventurous, risk-taking thief, you wouldn't classify him as an everyday sociopath because by stealing from the rich and giving to the poor he was following a moral standard that he chose to live by to benefit others. There's a sense of social justice in his actions.

HE'S COLD

Sociopaths don't experience emotions the same way as other people. They don't really "get" what human suffering is, nor do they care—often they are amused by it. Expressions of compassion or concern are liable to seem silly, sentimental, and overly sensitive to this type of guy.

After a month or two, forty-year-old social worker Tara began to notice this coldness in her boyfriend Rick, a forty-five-year-old computer programmer. His reaction to some specific events tipped her off. In one case, Tara's friend lost control of the car on black ice and hit a fence; her friend was hospitalized for three days. Rick's first reaction was, "What a dumb ass."

Another time, Rick and Tara went to his friends' dinner party. The husband was so verbally abusive to his wife during dinner that it caused a heart-wrenching scene, bringing the wife to tears. Rick's reaction: "That was awesome!"

The more coldness Rick seemed to show, the more Tara tried to find warmth in him. During a state-of-the-relationship discussion a few months down the road, she overtly prodded him about his feelings toward her.

"Do you really love me?" Tara demanded.

"Well, yeah," was Rick's underwhelming reply. "Everybody loves his girlfriend, right?"

Clearly, this was not the answer Tara was looking for. She recognized that there was no "I love you" coming from inside him. Rather it was something that he witnessed other people doing—loving their girlfriends.

Watching love from the sidelines rather than feeling it himself caused Rick to miss something in the translation. People fall in love because of specific qualities that they possess. Not everybody in a relationship is expected to be in love.

Emotional incongruities are dead giveaways for the sociopathic temperament. But you really have to pay attention. Because the sociopath recognizes that he doesn't experience feelings of empathy, joy, or love in the same way as other people and senses he's different in a negative way, he becomes a quick study of human nature as well as a student of acting. Sociopaths can act quite charming and empathic when they choose to.

Remember, though, the sociopathic version of empathy goes only to a certain point and then stops colder than a dead fish. There may be empathy in the sense of *understanding* another person's feelings, yet they lack the ability to *connect* with those feelings. In other words, everyday sociopaths may recognize or comprehend your feelings, but they don't feel for you. The acting skills really come into play here, as they must pretend to identify with your emotions—often with malevolent intent.

Yet acting, even if it's good acting, is not authentic. It's like a man who is blind from birth trying to pretend that he can see. He doesn't have an internal frame of reference for what vision actually is, so he has to go by secondhand accounts instead. How long do you think this guy could fool you?

Really, the sociopath isn't much different. Even if his façade seems charming and endearing and wonderful, you may catch something that's off at some point. Maybe he's laying it on a little salesmanlike and thick. Maybe the way he expresses himself seems overly clichéd or fake. Whatever it is, that façade will crack eventually. The anger, contempt, and callousness will emerge.

HE USES PEOPLE

Sociopaths are parasitic by nature. They use people and are good at it. Their attitude in any relationship—romantic or otherwise—is: "What can you do for me?" If you can't do anything for him, you can count on being cut loose sooner rather than later.

If you suspect you're being used by someone with sociopath tendencies, stop and think about how he might be benefiting from your relationship. Is there a financial benefit for him to be going out with you? Is it sex?

Because of their faulty emotional structure, sociopaths have very empty inner lives. Often they like to have a female hanging around to try to fill that void. They might want to own you for a while so that you can take care of their neediness. Unfortunately, it's endless neediness that can't be eliminated.

Sociopaths do form attachments, but they're not healthy ones. They have no emotional mechanism that allows for warm, in-depth attachments and intimacy.[4] Instead it's a sponging, leechlike bond in which they want to come out on top.

Sydney, a thirty-one-year-old chemical engineer, understands that Chris, a struggling actor, takes one thousand times more than he gives, yet she still chooses to live with it. She sees that it's a pattern of behavior that he does not only with her but also with friends and family.

At first, Sydney thought it was great Chris had such a close relationship with his brother. Then she realized that he became close only when he needed money. Otherwise, he never had much to do with him.

Chris's friends were nothing more than bodies who accompanied him to various activities. He didn't know much about what was going on in their lives, nor did he care.

He also developed a parasitic attachment to Sydney. In the beginning he took pleasure in how much she loved him. He liked how easy it was to take advantage of her in every possible way. There were nights when Chris didn't come home, and there were days when he didn't say more than two words to an increasingly sad Sydney. Yet he knew that she would continue to put up with it.

Once Sydney tried to leave Chris, and it threw him into an actual frenzy. His extreme reaction wasn't because he loved her in the way most people love, but because the object that he'd grown accustomed to having around and using was gone (and not by his choosing). Chris turned on the charm for about five minutes and managed to coax her back. Sydney and Chris are still together and nothing has changed—except now he has a baby with another woman.

HE'S GUILT FREE

"Right" and "wrong" are empty words and don't mean much to a sociopath. Our friendly sociopath lives in a moral vacuum in which guilt and shame have no role. A man without remorse is dangerous. He can carry out antisocial acts such as theft or violence and not even blink. He can be in a relationship, treat the woman despicably, and not think twice about it.

Having a "relationship" with this guy is always going to be tenuous at best. Because he has no internal character compass to stop him from doing things he shouldn't do, he generally succumbs to his whims. If anything that seems better to him pops up, he'll walk away without compunction.

HE'S MANIPULATIVE

An everyday sociopath doesn't come out and say, "I want to take all I can from you and then throw you away at will." He attempts to lure you in at first. He's quite the con man.

Twenty-seven-year-old Patrick, a successful stockbroker, got glee not only out of conning women into bed but also from telling them all the little con games he used to pull on other people when he was younger. If there were any current cons he was pulling on Wall Street, he must have kept those to himself.

He became outright animated telling the story of how he and his friend stole liquor and sometimes drugs from other people's parties to stock his own. Patrick was the front man who distracted his mark with friendly banter while his friend reached and grabbed.

Patrick also ran a good scam at college by collecting money from his fellow students for a fake charity and pocketing the contributions. His justification was that he needed the money more than they did.

It's possible that these episodes could be a case of youthful mischievousness and not indicative of sociopathic tendencies, but they're big red flags—especially if these little cons occur in conjunction with the other sociopathic tendencies indicated. Patrick's sense of entitlement and lack of remorse with regard to stealing from his peers are particularly distressing.

The typical sociopath cons and manipulates you by lying like a dog! In some cases, he may commit lies of omission in which he skillfully leaves out pertinent information that you should know. In other cases, he flat-out lies to your face.

Another path to manipulation is through preying on your weaknesses. Remember, the sociopath is a student of human nature. He is intensely aware of people's moods and emotional states, although he doesn't have a very rich emotional life of his own. He knows how to find your Achilles' heel and use it to manipulate you as he sees fit.[5]

Ted Bundy, the notorious good-looking and charming serial killer of women, was a master manipulator. An example of sociopathy at its predatory extreme, Bundy's behavior can provide us with some insight that may help in the future.

In *The Stranger Beside Me: Ted Bundy*, Ann Rule makes an interesting connection. She notes that a commonality between his victims was preoccupation. Something had gone "awry" in all of the women's lives around the time they were preyed upon by Bundy, which served to distract them from his true intentions. She hypothesizes that Bundy, like an animal on the hunt, smelled their vulnerability and weakness. Somehow he sensed that these particular women would be the best targets.[6]

With a sociopathic serial killer, the difference between being distracted or attentive could mean the difference between life and death. With everyday sociopaths, distraction and vulnerability could result in a horrific relationship experience, as well as possible physical harm.

How do you go about protecting yourself from a predator who can smell vulnerability like a wild animal can sniff out fear? The first thing to do is be aware of what makes you vulnerable, because everyone, no matter who she is, experiences times of weakness. Following are some emotional states or situations that can make people raw and exposed, causing a loss of focus:

- depression
- anxiety
- loneliness and the strong desire for a relationship
- the postbreakup period
- grief
- feeling overwhelmed and pulled in a million different directions
- intoxication
- multitasking to the extreme
- low self-esteem—feeling you're just not good enough
- the false sense that this guy may be your one last shot at happiness
- denial

Recognition is extremely important, so if you can identify when you're in these vulnerable states, that's excellent! Identify your weakness in order to employ the appropriate defenses against the everyday sociopath.

You can defend yourself by working through your weaknesses. Profiling can also be a great protector.

Profiling can help you gain objectivity. When a sociopath wants you, he stretches out his tentacles and entwines himself deep inside you, so that, at times, you may not know your own mind. By profiling, not only do you know your own mind, but you can better get into his mind. It's a defensive shield from his groping tentacles and an offensive action to get to know him instead.

Be Your Own Lie Detector

AS SURE AS THE SUN SHINES, everyday sociopaths will lie. Because practiced liars with little conscience are good at lying and are skilled at fooling people, they are difficult to catch in a lie. Therefore, over-confidence regarding your ability to detect lies can be one of the biggest missteps. Never underestimate your opponent!

There are, however, ways you can attempt to stack the odds in your favor. Being aware that people aren't always going to be as truthful with you as you are with them is a big step. That's not to say you should assume every man you talk to is a liar. Profiling doesn't promote being cynical; it helps you become aware. Here are few ways to spot a liar.

GOOD EYE CONTACT MAY MEAN GOOD LIAR

It seems counterintuitive, but sometimes liars actually give you more eye contact than truth tellers. Maybe it's because they know you're looking for giveaway eyes. Maybe they realize that women may not trust a man who can't look them straight in the eye. What-ever the reason, among "Machiavellian types" in particular, eye contact may intensify during deception.[7] (The term "Machiavel-lian" usually refers to people who don't care about whom they hurt as long as they reach their goal, whether it is power, money, or something else. In fact, these types often get a sadistic pleasure in watching others squirm as they plunder and pillage their way to the top.)

MONA LISA SMILE?

It's long been suspected that Mona Lisa has something to hide. A lot of the controversy lies behind that striking, ambiguous smile.

So what *lies* behind your date's smile? Well, if it's an "enjoyment smile," maybe only the thrill of being with you! Big and bright "enjoyment smiles" involve both the lips and the eyes.[8] You'll also notice the crinkles at the corners of his eyes. "Enjoyment smiles" last less than five seconds.

In contrast, what are called "masking smiles" tend to last longer . . . the longer to deceive you with! These are the smiles that may be indicative of a cover-up. Watch for smiles that don't involve the eyes, have a hint of negative emotion in the muscle movement, or are more pronounced toward one side of the face (a crooked smile).[9]

A BLINK, NOT A WINK

The stress of deception can set a liar all aflutter—his lids, that is. As the burden of a lie weighs upon its perpetrator, his blink rate may go up.[10]

THOU DOTH PROTEST TOO MUCH

When people feel the need to draw your attention to their truthfulness and trustworthiness during a conversation, that should give you pause.[11] Statements such as, "You know I would never lie to you" or "I'm not lying," are often said with the goal of deception. So are qualifiers like "honestly," "frankly," and "truthfully," which seem prematurely defensive.

Ask yourself why he is compelled to assert his honesty. Could it simply be an innocuous phrase he's in the habit of using, or could it be a clue to a noxious personality?

CASUAL LYING

It's easy to assume a liar will give himself away by being obviously nervous, because a person who is visibly edgy can seem like he has something to hide. Sometimes he might be stretching the truth, because the stress of lying can make people appear uptight, fidgety, and uneasy.

But our everyday sociopath is extremely clever. He knows that if he appears nervous, you might suspect him of telling tall tales. To counteract the nerves, he acts casual! Liars frequently slump in their chairs and sprawl out on the couch in order to pretend they're comfortable.[12]

Be particularly mindful if he's acting laid-back during a tension-filled situation. For example, during a first date conversation, it's natural to feel nervous. If this guy is slouching and cavalier and behaving like "the Dude" incarnate, something may be up.

INCONSISTENCIES BETWEEN NONVERBAL CUES AND WORDS

There are many inconsistencies that can blow the lid off deceptions. An important one is the discrepancy between verbal cues and non-verbal cues. When body language and facial expressions don't jibe with the spoken word, there could be more to the interaction than meets the ear.

In counseling sessions, therapists often make note of these incongruities because they could signal areas that need to be explored further. It doesn't necessarily mean that the client is trying to outright deceive the therapist, but it could signal that the client is trying to conceal something from the therapist and maybe also from himself or herself.

At times, part of the therapeutic process is to call attention to incongruent words and behaviors. If the client walks in and says, "Yeah, I have a really happy marriage," but looks like his dog just died while he's saying it, there's probably more to explore there.

The following are a few questions that can draw your attention toward verbal/nonverbal inconsistencies:

- Does he say he's not angry while trying to suppress a look that could kill?
- Does a momentary smirk come across his face as he feigns concern over something?
- Does he say he's a gentleman but then at dinner paw you to the point that you feel uncomfortable?
- Does he say no while his head nods yes?
- Does his tone of voice convey a different message from his words?

INCONSISTENCIES OF STORY

Men who lie eventually dig themselves into a hole. They may forget their lies and contradict themselves during another conversation with you, they may put forth a bunch of facts that don't add up, or they may leave out information, causing strange gaps in the story they're conveying.

You've probably found that most good liars try to keep their stories as close to the truth as possible and diverge into deception only at certain key points. Even so, there may be a moment in time when they trip themselves up. Don't let that moment pass you by.

When a man's story is inconsistent, you usually feel confused. Even though he has explained something about his life in detail, you still may be thinking, "Hang on a minute, what'd he just say?" In these situations, there's nothing wrong and everything right with asking for clarification. If after clarification something still doesn't ring right, he's either a muddle-brain or else it's a case of willful obfuscation.

Condi had this problem with Devon regarding his education. Devon always mentioned a bunch of different schools he transferred to and from, but she never could get a handle on where he actually got his degree. After reaching the frustration point, followed by careful prodding, Condi learned he did *not* graduate from college, even though he led her to believe he had a Harvard MBA.

Be aware when a man tries to overdetail you to death. And if something seems out of whack, contradictory, or incongruous, don't be afraid to call him on it!

IT'S NOT *ME*, IT'S *YOU* WHO ISN'T GETTING IT!

A central premise about everyday sociopaths is that they prey on weaknesses. In order to sell you on a lie, this guy is going to scan you like an X-ray machine and find your soft spot. The really scary part is that he may do it so well—in such an nonconfrontational, nonthreatening way—that you don't notice it . . . unless you're profiling, that is!

Start paying attention if he tries to nullify his lies with tricks like these:

> *"No, what I said last week was . . ."*

Here he's attempting to call your memory into question. He wants to make you doubt what you heard. If he's successful, you're going to start thinking that you're ready for the Alzheimer's unit. If you're profiling, you won't be easily swayed. Write things down, if need be, so that you have concrete proof of your accurate memory.

> *"Oh, I was just kidding. Where's your sense of humor?"*

With this statement, he's playing on the suggestion that you're not a fun, cool person, "You're just so serious all the time." Well, forget that! Who wants to be fun and cool when someone's lying to her?

"You misunderstood . . . that's not what I told you."

After more than a few "you misunderstoods," you may begin to think you're going crazy or losing some IQ points, which is exactly what the liar wants. He wants you more focused on your own intelligence and sanity than his lying.

Armed with these liars' tricks of the trade, this guy is ready to talk his way through deceit. How skillfully he can turn the conversation around so that you think you're wrong about the facts, when actually you're right. And what about the way he tries to create distance from the lie by distracting you with your own weaknesses?

Of course, in all relationships there are misunderstandings and miscommunications. That's normal. The difference is that with a liar, you have a feeling that the misunderstandings and the miscommunications are abnormal. You're left with a sense of discomfort after conversations that incorporates doubt about him as well as self-doubt.

Lovesick over a Sociopath? Better Run Like Hell!

PERHAPS YOU'VE PROFILED a past or current boyfriend as an everyday sociopath. He has the boredom, the coldness, the exploitation, the lack of remorse, as well as the manipulation and lies.

If this relationship is in the past, you're in good shape. His initial bad-boy appeal will be replaced by, "Ewww, what was I thinking?" If you're still looking for a little "edge" in a man, you're interested only in edge that's tempered by compassion, sensitivity, and morality. You've profiled and made the choice never to get cut on a cold, hard, everyday-sociopath edge again.

However, if you're in a relationship with a guy like this, or if you happen to cross paths with a guy like this, get out of the relationship as soon as possible. Don't take a chance: Run like hell.

Is Your Guy Anxiety Ridden and Stressed Out?

IF YOUR DATE IS STRESSED OUT or anxious, he might not let on to his emotional state in the same way that you would. Studies have shown that men don't express their fear as much as women. When fearful, women report that they tend to cry and freeze up, convey their fright with more intensity, and give more facial cues to their fear than men.[1] But just because men don't express these emotions it doesn't mean they don't experience them.

Men turn to substances like alcohol or nicotine more than women do as a way to endure anxiety-provoking situations rather than avoid them.[2] This means that a man is more likely to cope by self-medicating, which is not an effective solution. Drinking doesn't necessarily reduce anxiety in the short run, yet many people believe it does. In the long run, drinking may actually exacerbate anxiety! Have you ever been with a man who tended to drink, smoke, or use other drugs particularly when he was anxious or stressed?

To find out if the guy you're with is wigged out by worry, you may have to look a little harder and, through profiling, dig a little deeper than you would with one of your female friends. A friend would probably lay it all out on the table, whereas a boyfriend may bottle it up inside. We all know that once the cork pops—which it inevitably will—there will be an explosion.

To prevent his anxiety and stress from exploding, you need to identify and address it. For one thing, a man who has major job stress, stress from a previous trauma, or other anxiety disorders may not be ready to commit to you unless he has dealt with these issues. Also, you want to know how he manages his stress and anxiety. Does he try to mitigate these feelings through effective coping strategies, or does he constantly take his stuff out on you?

Profiling for anxiety and stress can help you be prepared, be supportive, *and* be less anxious and stressed out yourself! Not to mention, he'll more than appreciate the fact that someone "gets" what he's going through.

Stress vs. Anxiety

STRESS IS A PSYCHOLOGICAL AND PHYSICAL reaction to the obstacles or stressors that life places before us. In contrast, anxiety can be defined as "a general feeling of apprehension about possible danger. . . . We are anticipating some dreadful thing happening that is not entirely predictable from our actual circumstances." While stress is a reaction to specific obstacles, anxiety is a worry about what could happen.[3]

STRESS HAPPENS!

Unfortunately, people don't always get what they want when they want it, nor can they always make things go away when they want.

When faced with these less-than-ideal circumstances (debt, family conflict, time constraints, poor health, etc.) or other life changes (moving, a new job, etc.), individuals experience "adjustive demands" that are stress provoking.

Of real interest with regard to stress and stressing is the Social Readjustment Rating Scale, which is a measure of stress buildup over time.[4] You can find the test online (www.ucs.umn.edu/lasc/handouts/socialreadjustment.html), and it's a great way to see how much stress you and your guy might be experiencing. The test includes many life events, which are assigned numbers called "life change units." The more stressful the life event, the more life change units it gets. The following are some examples from the original version of the test:

- death of a spouse/significant other = 100
- divorce = 73 (the second highest)
- marriage = 50
- getting fired = 47
- sex problems = 39
- change in work responsibilities = 29
- dieting/change of eating habits = 15
- christmas = 12

As you can see from this short list, stress isn't always caused by a negative event. Marriage gets a big 50 life change units.

If we don't take measures to cope with stress successfully, it can really take over. For instance, when past trauma intrudes into the present, it can lead to major dysfunction, individually and in relationships. Also, when someone begins to feel paralyzed and weighed down by life events, that definitely fits the bill of being overstressed and is cause for action.

ANXIETY

Anxiety is dread about all the possible things that can go wrong in our lives. It's hard to see the bright side of anxiety, but there is one. Having an appropriate amount of anxiety gets people motivated and in gear. For example, if a man had absolutely no anxiety about going on a first date, he might not be driven to look his best and tell his most entertaining stories. In more critical situations, anxiety makes us safety conscious, so we wear seat belts or lock our doors.

Anxiety becomes a problem when it's out of proportion to the situation. If he'd rather die than give a speech, that's out of proportion. If he's on a well-constructed high-rise terrace and feels like he's being sucked off the edge and will plummet to the ground, that's out of proportion. If he dreads waking up in the morning because he's worried about every single bad thing that *could* happen, that's out of proportion.

In a British study,[5] the four most common indicators of anxiety were identified as

- tiredness
- sleep problems
- irritability
- worry

Remember, a man may not let his worry show. The key is to pick up the other signs: tiredness, sleep problems, and irritability. He's less likely to be able to hide these things. Once you notice he isn't sleeping right and seems touchy, do some investigating to see if worry is part of the package.

As you assess the situation, you can choose a direct or an indirect route to get at the issue. Psychotherapists use both types of approaches depending on the situation and the client. In the following examples, stick with A statements if you're going for a less question-oriented approach. Use both A statements and B questions if you want to be more direct.

A	B
I feel bad that you woke up last night and couldn't get back to sleep . . .	Was there anything on your mind that kept you awake?
It seems like you're set off more easily today than usual . . .	Is there anything you want to talk to me about?
You look like I did last week—like every ounce of energy was drained out of you. The reason I felt that way was because I was so worried about starting that new project at work . . .	Could worrying about something be making you tired?

There are a number of types of both stress and anxiety, including job stress, post-traumatic stress, social anxiety, obsessive-compulsive tendencies, phobias, generalized anxiety, and panic attacks.

Job Stress

A MAN'S JOB CAN BE an important part of his identity, so much a part of his day-to-day life that there's no surprise it's a major source of stress. In the United States, 45 percent of both men and women in responsible positions report being highly job stressed, while 15 percent state they have chronic depression because of excessive and unremitting job demands.[6]

The major causes of job stress have been revealed through research studies.[7] During discussions with your guy, see if he brings up one or more of the following. If so, there's a good chance he's under stress, although he might not admit it right away.

Does He Talk About . . .

- an unworkable workload?
- unrealistic deadlines and time pressures?
- managers with a bad attitude?
- managers with bad interpersonal skills?
- dysfunctional relationships with coworkers?
- disagreeable client contacts?
- job insecurity?
- general job pressures?
- harassment?

If he alludes to some of these things but doesn't go into detail about them, try employing some of the skills in Chapter 2, "Getting into His Head and into His Heart," designed to get your date to open up. Chances are that although he is keeping these issues inside, he needs to get them out.

Post-Traumatic Stress Disorder

POST-TRAUMATIC STRESS DISORDER, or PTSD, came into cultural awareness during the period of the Vietnam War, in recognition of mental-health issues that veterans were facing. Now, in the wake of 9/11, the war in Iraq, and terror around the world, PTSD has a new face. Yet PTSD isn't a diagnosis that is given only to those traumatized by war and terrorism.

Any person exposed to a traumatic stressor and feeling "intense fear, helplessness, or horror" at the time could be at risk for PTSD.[8] Such stressors include but are not limited to the following:

- emotional, physical, or sexual abuse
- witnessing or experiencing a heinous crime
- natural disasters, for example, earthquakes, tornados, floods, tsunamis
- the diagnosis of a terminal illness
- hostage situations
- having your life or the lives of those that you love threatened
- a serious car accident
- growing up or living in a violence-ridden environment

If the man in your life has been exposed to one or more of these stressors, he's likely to be filled with hurt and pain. If he is still dealing with thoughts and feelings unleashed by the trauma, he may not be able to move forward with you, because the past still haunts him.

According to the experts, "re-experiencing" and "avoidance" are generally considered the two primary responses to trauma and are central in the diagnosis of PTSD.[9]

Re-experiencing the traumatic event means that he may be reliving that event over and over again in different ways; avoidance is the attempt to block out the event. Re-experiencing and avoidance are not mutually exclusive; on the contrary, they can be parallel processes.

Re-experiencing can include invasive thoughts and images, anxiety, anger, aggression, nightmares, flashbacks, and heightened physiological reactions to reminders of the trauma. Signs of avoidance include loss of memory regarding the trauma, emotional numbing, and avoiding situations that serve as reminders of the trauma.[10]

In relationships, you'll notice that someone who has experienced trauma can have acute interpersonal struggles that may result in estrangement.[11] For example, a man could feel like you'll never understand what he has been through. Or he could cut himself off from all of his feelings, including the ones reserved for you. Maybe he feels so guilty about some aspect of the trauma that he believes he doesn't deserve happiness.

Many people who have experienced trauma can get bogged down in unhealthy relationship patterns such as "pursue/withdraw" and "attack/defend." One study found that combat veterans with PTSD tended to have relationships that were less close, less emotionally expressive, and more argumentative and violent than those of veterans without PTSD.[12]

In our world, trauma is not uncommon, which makes dealing with the effects of trauma so all-important. It must be worked through! Therapy and support groups are a good beginning when it comes to working through PTSD.

The Shy or Socially Anxious Guy

BEING SHY OR SOCIALLY ANXIOUS is one of the biggest roadblocks in dating. Approximately 30 to 40 percent of Americans identify themselves as having a shy disposition.[13] That amounts to a significant portion of the dating population!

Shy and socially anxious are grouped together because the two concepts are very similar. Here are a few things shy people and people with social anxiety have in common:[14]

NEGATIVE THOUGHTS IN SOCIAL SITUATIONS. Thinking everyone else is much better, being self-conscious and self-critical, believing everyone is standing in harsh judgment.

PHYSIOLOGICAL AROUSAL IN SOCIAL SITUATIONS. Blushing, sweating, rapid heartbeat, shaking, restlessness, hyperventilation, etc.

THE PROPENSITY TO AVOID SOCIAL SITUATIONS. Turning down invitations, avoiding dating situations, never approaching anyone to ask her out.

A LACK OF SOCIAL SKILLS. Having a hard time starting conversations, not knowing what to do or say in new social situations, staying in wallflower mode during a party.

One difference between shyness and social anxiety is that shyness is more common than social anxiety and tends to impair the person less.[15] In other words, social anxiety tends to be more severe than shyness.

In terms of the dating pool, most likely the shy ones are only occasionally (or perhaps rarely) dipping their feet into the pool without frequently jumping in and getting wet.

Because shy guys avoid social situations, you're not as likely to meet them. Since they lack some social skills, even if a shy guy has the courage to approach you, he may be awkward and be very self-conscious. You may think a guy seems stuck-up because he's not talking to anyone, but he may be shy and having negative thoughts about himself, like "I'm such a dork."

To help reduce this anxious feeling during social events, many men self-medicate with alcohol. The problem is that drinking may reduce social inhibitions but not necessarily anxiety. In essence, it's a quick fix that might not really fix anything. It certainly doesn't alleviate any underlying issues. Moreover, relying on alcohol as a crutch could spiral into a nasty addiction, not to mention more social embarrassment than anticipated!

Taking all the effects of shyness and anxiety into account, it's not surprising that there is a big impact on relationship patterns. One study showed that American and Swedish males who were shy as children married later and became parents later than their nonshy male counterparts.[16] Interestingly, the American and Swedish females who were shy as children did not marry later or become parents later than their female peers. Perhaps this discrepancy is related to the higher expectations on men to initiate conversations and ask for dates.

This means that there are a lot of shy men out there whom you may be missing out on. If you unintentionally dismiss all the shy and socially anxious men from your dating repertoire, you're severely reducing your dating pool.

Through profiling you'll come to realize that some men who seem standoffish are actually shy or anxious. Unfortunately, it's not always easy to tell which is which. Profiling in these cases might require you to take a bit more initiative. If you know people who know him, you can ask, "Is he shy?"

If you don't know anyone who knows him, you have to shed a little shyness of your own and use your profiling skills, such as open questioning (see Chapter 2), to draw him out. Don't bang your head against a brick wall if this guy doesn't end up cracking. You simply want to create an open demeanor so that the more shy types are not as afraid to let themselves open up to you.

Obsessive-Compulsive Tendencies

REMEMBER JACK NICHOLSON'S dogmatic yet eventually lovable character in the movie *As Good as It Gets*? Mr. Udall's obsessive-compulsive behavior led him to never using a bar of soap more than once and practically scalding his hands washing them with extremely hot water. Not to mention that he avoided cracks in the sidewalk, had a ritualistic way of locking his doors, and needed everything in order and just so.

One endearing quality of the character is that Mr. Udall was self-motivated to manage his symptoms and in the end was able to enter into a relationship with Helen Hunt's character, Carol. In some ways, this is one of Hollywood's more realistic love stories. It's about loving someone while at the same time coping with and managing mental-health issues, rather than waving a therapeutic wand and making it all better.

If the man you're dating has obsessive-compulsive tendencies as extreme as Mr. Udall's, perhaps he has obsessive-compulsive disorder. Or he may have some ritualistic behaviors you've noticed. Is he a neurotic neat freak? Does the same thought pop in his mind over and over?

Everyone has ritualistic or habitual thoughts and behaviors to some degree. That's why it's important to look at the frequency, intensity, and duration of the rituals and see if they reach the level of obsession and compulsion.

An obsession is defined as "an intrusive, repetitive thought, image, or impulse that is unacceptable or unwanted and gives rise to subjective resistance," whereas a compulsion is a "repetitive, stereotyped act."[17] Both obsessions and compulsions seem to be tied together and often coexist.

People experiencing obsessions and/or compulsions have some idea that they're being "senseless" and a little off-the-wall. Yet, although they are aware that they're being obsessive-compulsive, they find it hard to stop. Clearly, there is a great deal of anxiety associated with these tendencies.

The following are other types of thoughts and behaviors that may tip you off to a man's obsessive-compulsive proclivities:

- He arranges his books and CDs in alphabetical order.
- He finds it necessary to add up license plate numbers in his head.
- There's a specific place for everything in his home, and he doesn't want anything touched or moved.
- He keeps checking and rechecking to see that the lights are off or the windows are closed.
- He's so freaked out by germs that he's tempted to pour antiseptic all over you when you have a cold.

While plenty of people alphabetize their books, CDs, and DVDs and keep a neat home, the difference between organized and obsessive lies in the answer to a key question: How much are the obsessions and/or compulsions affecting his life? For example, does he get so upset when you disrupt his rituals that it affects the relationship? Are his nonsensical ceremonies wasting a good portion of the day? If so, they need to be dealt with individually and within the context of the relationship. Again, therapists and self-help manuals can provide him (and you) with techniques to aid in controlling these out-of-control "habits."

Phobias

A PHOBIA IS ESSENTIALLY an irrational fear. When individuals become consumed by fear of a particular thing or a particular circumstance, they are usually aware that they are overreacting—but at the same time they seem incapable of overriding that fear.

Common phobias include fear of flying, heights, elevators, doctors, dentists, and all kinds of animals, such as snakes and mice. Then there are the more esoteric phobias, including dust, caterpillars, bras, wood, grass, dirty laundry, and envelopes!

If he does have phobias, you need to profile to what degree they affect him (and will ultimately affect your relationship). How much does his out-of-proportion fear affect his life and his daily functioning? If he engages in all sorts of verbal, mental, and physical gymnastics to avoid the feared object or circumstance, then it's probably getting to phobic levels.

These avoidance tactics can act as a cue that he may be phobic. For example, a man who is phobic about water might not want to come out and say to you that he feels like curling up in a ball every time he's around a pool.

Instead, he mumbles, gets defensive, and changes the subject every time you mention swimming. Using your profiling skills to reveal phobias in these situations enhances communication, brings you closer together in the relationship, and helps him deal with his fear.

Along with the degree of the phobia, the type of phobia(s) he has also greatly influence how much it affects his life and whether or not he seeks professional help for it. If the guy is crippled by a fear of flying yet is required to fly for work, that's a problem needing a solution.

On the other hand, if he has a phobia of white tigers, it's unlikely to have a negative effect on his daily life, unless he's in Vegas or in the wild. The amount of attention you give to coping with the phobia depends on the amount of distress and inconvenience it causes him as well as your relationship.

Generalized Anxiety Disorder

GENERALIZED ANXIETY DISORDER, or GAD, is perhaps the most basic anxiety disorder because, at the core, its definition is constant worry.[18] Whereas a phobia is anxiety that is directed toward something specific, generalized anxiety is worry over everything and anything. It's so free-floating that the anxiety is easily transferred from one thing to another. People with GAD usually find something to be worried about.

To assess whether or not your date is afflicted with GAD, consider the degree of his anxiety and how much it's impairing his day-to-day functioning. Also take note if he has a family history of significant anxiety, was fearful as a child, and has problems concentrating on tasks.[19]

Panic Attacks

DURING A PANIC ATTACK, which includes chest pain and shortness of breath, it's not unusual for people to think that they're dying or that something undefined yet unspeakable is about to happen. Panic attacks may also be accompanied by tremendous fear or uneasiness, increased heart rate, shaking and sweating, a sense of "going crazy" or losing control, as well as the desire to "escape."[20]

The "attack" part of panic attack is quite appropriate since it comes on suddenly and lasts for a limited period of time. Sometimes, the attack is triggered by a specific event. Other times, it can seem to come out of the blue. However, research studies have shown that the seemingly out-of-the-blue attacks may actually be traceable to negative life events or thoughts happening around the panic period.[21]

Have you ever been out with a man who experiences panic attacks? Even if you were, it's something he's not likely to talk about, particularly right away.

There are elements of a "panic-prone" personality that you might be able to detect. Individuals prone to panic attacks tend to have a high need for control together with a feeling of being threatened by loss of control or change. Additionally, they are often compulsive, with overly high expectations for themselves and others. It is also interesting that panic-prone people may be avoiders. That is, rather than bringing their feelings to the forefront, they may steer clear of potential triggers, channel them into activities, or repress them altogether.[22]

Wait Before *You* Panic!

THE RANGE OF ANXIETY DISORDERS is quite large. It encompasses issues that include obsessive-compulsive thoughts and behaviors, panic attacks, phobias, post-traumatic stress, social anxiety, and generalized excessive worry.

Interestingly, if you do have an anxious man on your hands, he might also be highly intelligent. Some anxiety-related disorders such as obsessive-compulsive disorder have been shown to occur more among people with higher education levels and higher IQ than the general population.[23] Maybe it takes a bright person to think up a wide range of issues to worry about!

Many of the anxiety disorders have a good cure rate with therapy, sometimes coupled with medication. That's one of the reasons why it's important to spot the signs in your anxious man, so that he can get help and not cause you to have an anxiety attack!

Forecasting the Dark Days of Depression and High Pressure of Mania

PICTURE YOURSELF WALKING into the middle of a conversation about a person who has been sad and depressed. Everybody is worried because this person has appeared unhappy for so long. You don't know whom they're talking about and gender hasn't been mentioned. Do you assume the subject of the conversation is a man or a woman?

Traditionally, the automatic assumption would have been that it was a woman. If the word "tearful" had come up in the conversation, then most of us would assume a woman was the subject of discussion. Depression, however, strikes men just as vehemently—and just as insidiously—as women. Depression can be more deadly for men, they actually kill themselves at four times the rate of women.[1]

Both men and women experience depression in similar fashion and suffer with the same symptoms. But there are gender differences. Men don't always wear the obvious signs of depression on their sleeves, and the signs they do show may be misleading. A man who appears to be angry might actually be depressed. It's important to be able to spot the signs of masculine depression because by acknowledging the warning signs, it may be possible to help ease a man's pain and maybe improve a relationship.

How do you know when you have a clinically depressed man on your hands, as opposed to one who is experiencing an average life funk? If you are dating someone who is depressed, what does it mean for the relationship? What avenues are open to you if you want to work through it with him?

Down, Down, Down

IN GENERAL, DEPRESSION CAN BE described as pervasive negativity or a weighty pessimism that clouds over a person's life. Elizabeth Wurtzel, author of *Prozac Nation*, describes it this way: "Slowly, over the years, the data will accumulate in your heart and mind, a computer program for total negativity will build into your system, making life feel more and more unbearable."[2] The way she puts it, depression is a process, not something static. Negativity invades every thought and feeling so that a person develops pessimistic ideas about oneself and about the world.

With the negativity, a sense of helplessness and hopelessness takes over. What does this mean for a man in today's society? Although gender roles are dramatically shifting toward equality, there is still a socialization process that emphasizes strength and self-assurance in men. The helplessness and hopelessness of depression is the opposite of this assertiveness and power.

Symptoms of Depression

RESEARCHERS HAVE IDENTIFIED several regularly reported symptoms by both men and women (I'll get to the list in a second) that can serve as a guide.[3] Because many people have or will experience some form of clinical depression—the lifetime probability of experiencing major depressive disorder is 10 percent to 25 percent for women and 5 percent to 12 percent for men[4]—it's likely that you may recognize some of these symptoms in yourself. If you see signs of depression in yourself, it's important to take action, just as you would want the man in your life to do.

Keep in mind that when psychotherapists are looking at a diagnosis of depression, a primary focus is the duration, intensity, and frequency of symptoms. Everybody has a bad day. The concern is when a bad day turns into a bad few weeks or a bad few years. If you or a man you are dating has experienced any of the following symptoms, depression could be a possibility.

APPETITE AND SLEEP CHANGES

Sleeping too much, sleeping too little, eating too much, and eating too little can all signal depression. Watch out for marked changes in appetite and weight or shifts in sleep patterns.

DYSPHORIA

The most common symptom of depression reported by both sexes is dysphoria, which is a general state of unhappiness. For dysphoric individuals, feelings of pleasure and contentment are replaced by melancholy and despair.

FATIGUE

The exhaustion that accompanies depression isn't the tired from a hard day's work or a hard day's play run-of-the-mill fatigue. It is a physical and psychological weariness that is often accompanied by a lack of motivation. A man experiencing depressive fatigue may not want to get out of bed or get off the couch. He appears listless and lacking in energy.

GUILT

Guilt is an interesting symptom of depression, because people don't always associate the two. The fact is that often a depressed man is filled with self-reproach. He might wallow in blame and shame about things that go wrong at work as well as in his relationships. The underlying thought process is, "It's all my fault. I'm a loser and can't do anything right."

It's definitely a vicious cycle, because as the depression causes lack of concentration, decreased productivity, and inattention to detail, the more the man sees himself as "messing up." This leads to extra guilt, further feeding the depression.

LACK OF CONCENTRATION

Depression is often accompanied by a lack of concentration. A depressed man might have problems getting absorbed into activities, be unable to attend fully to things like conversations, or seem a bit scattered, more forgetful, and less productive.

LOSS OF INTEREST

Loss of interest is a big one. Imagine that for an extended period of time you are unable to derive interest or joy from activities or people that used to be meaningful to you and used to make you happy. A depressed man doesn't get excited about anything or look forward to planned activities.

PSYCHOMOTOR CHANGES

You might notice a depressed man being restless or, at the opposite end of the spectrum, sluggish. Is he walking around like a paperweight? Does he seem like he can't get comfortable or relax?

THOUGHTS OF DEATH

Thoughts of death can be anything from, "I wish I wouldn't wake up in the morning" to "I'm going to buy a gun and shoot myself tomorrow." Therapists take every death thought seriously and are trained to take immediate action when a person has a suicidal plan and intent. A plan means the individual has a method and the means to carry out the suicide threat. Intent indicates that he or she is determined to go through with it.

If a client expresses a range of death thoughts, therapists usually work out a written "crisis agreement." A suicide crisis agreement is a contract signed by both the therapist and the client stating that the client promises not to harm himself or herself. Included in the agreement is a list of actions that the client promises to take in the event of suicidal thoughts, such as:

- contacting supportive friends and family
- calling his or her therapist or a crisis line for help
- calling 911
- getting involved in a calming activity that has worked in the past, such as going for a walk or going to a movie
- proactively removing possible means to suicide from his or her possession, such as giving guns or pills to a trusted support person

If a man in your life has ever confided death thoughts to you, it no doubt had to be a traumatic experience for you and him. Offering support and other avenues for him to get help are the most important things you can do.

Sometimes, however, in cases in which suicidal thoughts are involved (whether he has told you or kept them more or less a secret), it's hard to accept that you are not accountable for his actions. No one can take responsibility for another person's life. It's important to realize that even if you do everything you can do, he still may not choose to grab the life preserver. Tragically, you cannot force him to do so.

Man-Specific Depression

ALTHOUGH MEN AND WOMEN may experience depression in many of the same ways, there are some gender differences worth noting.

MEN GET ANGRY

Men's sad feelings may morph into angry feelings.[5] You notice that it doesn't take much to ignite his short fuse, and there are a number of ways he could blow. He could be snappy, cranky, verbally argumentative, or physically abusive.

MEN GET WASTED

Men who are depressed may self-medicate or attempt to numb the pain with drugs and/or alcohol.[6] This, does not mean, however that all men who drink or use drugs are depressed. Deciphering whether he uses it as a specific response to stress gives you a big clue. For example, if he says, "Everything's screwed up, I need a drink," that's more cause for concern with regard to depression than, "We're all going out and getting wasted at Mason's bachelor party tonight!"

MEN GET SELF-DESTRUCTIVE

Freud called it a death wish. Men who are depressed may engage in harmful behaviors like substance abuse, promiscuous sex, gambling, and high-risk physical activities.

MEN GET UNINTERESTED IN SEX

Although depressed men may not be as interested, research has shown that sexual activity does not decrease.[7] In this case, you might sense that the guy you're with isn't as involved or connected when you're having sex.

MEN GET TUNNEL VISION

As part of an effort to distract themselves from depression, men may compulsively pour their time into work or sports.[8] Spending time with a woman is a threat to getting the depression out in the open because she will probably want to talk about whatever is bothering him.

MEN GET WITHDRAWN

Men aren't prone to talk about their sad feelings with friends, family, or significant others.[9] They tend to retreat to their corners in an exaggerated show of independence because men are typically socialized to be self-reliant and do not want to be seen as "dependent" on others by asking for help. Drawing out why he has so tightly withdrawn takes a lot of skill and a lot of will on your part.

Depression and Your Relationship

IT'S NOT GOING to come as a surprise that a man's clinical depression takes a tough toll on relationships. The degree of his symptoms and his willingness to get help are major factors in working things out. Barry, a twenty-one-year-old student in a six-month relationship with his now pregnant girlfriend, realized that he had to get a grip on his sadness.

The stress of school, work, and a baby on the way plunged him into anger, guilt, self-hatred, and suicidal thoughts. He was also taking way too many chances on his motorcycle. Barry was very self-aware, especially for a guy his age, and had always recognized this depressive tendency in himself and knew it was dangerous. His grandfather and his uncle experienced similar "down moods," which led to suicide for both. Deciding not to take any chances, Barry sought therapy right away. Currently, he's better than stable, with regular therapy sessions and prescribed medication. His relationship with his girlfriend has remained intact.

Thirty-three-year-old Justin's case is more unfortunate, due to the severity of his depression combined with a lack of motivation to help himself. Like Barry, he had been seeing his girlfriend, Cara, for about six months. At the beginning of the relationship, Cara profiled Justin with depression. On the first date, she noticed how down he was on every aspect of his life, but she waited to see if it might be because of bad week at work or something else going on in his life. As she continued to date him, she saw that this mood wasn't going away.

Because of his sweet nature and a connection she felt between them, Cara didn't want to give up. At first she made suggestions that he get help and bought books on depression for him to read. When he ignored these overtures, she began to beg and plead for him to see a therapist. Justin refused, and his depression worsened.

One day Cara found pills that he had hidden under the couch. The next day, Justin said he might not "be around" for their date on the weekend. Another day, Justin sobbed about how tired he was of living. Poor Cara was emotionally torn beyond belief. Here was a guy she really liked, but this relationship was now affecting her psychological and physical health. Maybe he wasn't the right man for her, she thought.

Justin tried to break up with her several times, claiming he "wasn't worth it," which made Cara feel more guilty about possibly leaving him. Would he do something drastic if she did? Finally, based on his consistent refusal to get help, Cara ended the relationship. Before she left, she gave him several numbers for support and help, none of which Justin has used to this day.

It's important to be realistic about the effects of a man's depression on relationships. It doesn't work to shove it under the rug, like some men would prefer. There are also some women who think that as the relationship gets more committed, the problem will evaporate. They believe that love and marriage are the solution to a host of ills, which is definitely not the case. Research has shown that premarital dysphoria/depression in men is a predictor of future marital problems and conflicts.[10]

Many aspects of depression can lead to interpersonal conflict between you and him, including the possibility of anger and withdrawal. Moreover, low self-esteem that is part of depression can affect male and female interactions in a big, bad way. Depressed people often either need excessive reassurance to boost their self-esteem or else they goad others into giving them negative feedback to confirm their low self-esteem.[11] Sometimes, interactions are peppered with a confusing mix of both: a need to be told that they are good and a need to be told that they are bad.

In a relationship, this can leave you in a Catch-22 situation. You may reassure the guy a hundred times about your love for him, but the one time you make a suggestion or say something negative, you're left with, "I told you so. . . . I'm no good. . . . You don't love me. . . ." If he doesn't say it, he may be thinking it. A depressed man focuses on the negative, not the positive.

Again, as long as you recognize this pattern, there is hope and there is help. Individual therapy, group therapy, local support groups, medication, and education are all avenues for improvement. Many people are going to be touched by depression, whether it is in a family member, a significant other, or themselves. The past stigma is lifting. People don't want to hide; they want help.

Still, it's a tough and personal call if you profile someone with possible depression. The following list of questions will help you to think through some of the issues you will face when you're dating a depressed man:

- Does the depression seem more chronic or more situational? Is there an event that triggered the depressed mood, like a divorce or death in the family?
- Does he have depressed relatives? Suicides in the family?
- Does he have a self-destructive behavior pattern? Is he pulling you into it?
- Does he have a drug or alcohol problem along with the depression?
- Does he promise to get help, or does he get help?
- Does he threaten suicide often? Have there been suicide attempts?
- Does he verbally or physically abuse you?
- Do the depressed moods tend toward mild or toward severe?
- How does his depression affect your mental health?
- Does this relationship make *you* happy more often than not?

Clearly, as you're going through these questions, you can make a distinction between the better situations and the worse situations for you. A big factor is the state of your mental and physical health. If they are deteriorating while you are with this man, then it's not looking good. Also, the severity and frequency of his symptoms, together with his desire to get the depression under control, are big factors in the potential success of a relationship.

Up, Down, Up, Down

IF DEPRESSION IS A DOWNWARD mood spiral, bipolar disorder (aka manic depression) is a roller coaster of highs and lows. During the highs, a man might feel as if he can conquer the world, yet during the lows he might feel like the world has conquered him.

Throughout the ages, these dramatic mood shifts have been linked to the "artistic temperament" and creativity in general. In fact, there is some evidence that supports this perspective. Kay Jamison, author of *Touched with Fire: Manic-Depressive Illness and the Artistic Temperament,* discusses numerous famous artists, writers, and poets, such as Vincent Van Gogh, Percy Bysshe Shelley, and Edgar Allan Poe, who are thought to have suffered from bipolar disorder.

The theory goes that the manic phases of a bipolar person's life can be punctuated by intense productivity and creativity. Others, however, argue that bipolar disorder is overly romanticized and gets in the way of true productivity. Moreover, they say that artistry and mental illness have been too often falsely linked.

Whatever side of the argument you fall on, it's undeniable that bipolar disorder is a serious illness that has the potential to wreak havoc in the life of the man suffering from the disease, as well as those around him; hence the importance of identifying and seeking treatment for bipolar disorder.

SYMPTOMS OF BIPOLAR DISORDER

There are several varieties and offshoots of bipolar disorder, such as cyclothymia, which is a less severe form. There is also the mixed episode, in which a person experiences depression and mania at the same time. Rather than get bogged down in nuances, I'll look at some general cues that might be indicative of bipolar disorder.

A good way to understand the roller-coaster ride from mania to depression is by thinking of it as a change in drive states as well as mood.[12] You're bound to see abnormal fluctuations in normal drives such as eating, sleeping, sex, social interaction, and accomplishment seeking in someone with bipolar disorder.

A good description of the manic high is that "mood is expansive and emotion mercurial and euphoric, turning easily to irritability."[13] There's a lot of nervous, touchy energy floating around that can't be turned off at will. It's not always productive; some of that energy may be focused toward harmful or risky ventures. During manic stages, people may go on out-of-control shopping sprees, enter into chancy business deals, or get into inappropriate sexual situations.[14]

Even if the burst of energy is turned toward more practical and constructive pursuits, there's a good chance that they won't get finished. Therapists frequently see this. Bipolar clients come in gung-ho about a new career they're starting or a project they've just begun, and as soon as the manic phase subsides, so does the motivation to complete the task.

So how can you tell if your date is manic? People in a manic phase tend to be overly talkative and distractible.[15] A general hyperactivity in his behavior could be a heads-up. Still, this doesn't necessarily mean that the guy is manic; it could be anything from attention-deficit/hyperactivity disorder, to a drug-induced state, to simple nervousness at being out with an amazing woman like you! It is the generally cyclical nature and relative longevity of these symptoms that is key to distinguishing mania from some of these other causes.

BIPOLAR DISORDER AND YOUR RELATIONSHIP

Because bipolar disorder is a roller coaster of ups and downs, if you're in a relationship with someone who is bipolar, then be prepared for a very fast ride. As with depression, the health of your relationship with a bipolar person depends on the severity of the symptoms and his motivation to get help.

A typical problem encountered by couples with one bipolar partner is the nagging-to-get-treatment dilemma.[16] For example, if a man starts showing signs of entering into a manic phase, the woman, who has become familiar with the signs, recognizes it and suggests he take action. Maybe she wants to see if the doctor will adjust his medication; maybe she thinks he should visit his therapist more regularly. Whatever the case may be, she wants to take action and he doesn't, because he gets attached to this high phase and the feelings that go along with it.

The man then begins to see his significant other as a drag on his unnaturally good mood. Adding insult to injury, he may begin to feel that his partner and the mental health professionals are in cahoots, trying to ruin his high. Fortunately, it's been found that with the use of couples therapy techniques, this scenario can be, if not totally avoided, somewhat muted. Couples therapy techniques typically include education about the disorder, communication training, and coping strategies.

The irritability during mania can also pose a challenge to relationships. Irritability can shift to anger, and anger can all too quickly shift to rage. Sometimes a man channels his violent energy by screaming and shouting or sometimes by kicking a hole in the wall. The worst case is when his partner becomes the punching bag.

It's essential for a bad temper to be dealt with. Anger management classes can be helpful for men who need to learn appropriate ways to express rage and frustration.

Dealing with the often irritable high of mania is challenging enough, but bipolar disorder is also accompanied by depression. It can be tremendously stressful to watch someone experience different extreme sets of symptoms while in different mood states. It throws not only the man off balance, but those around him as well.

Whether it's the up, down, up, down of bipolar disorder or the down, down, down of depression, he's experiencing a disturbance of mood and it is serious. At the beginning of a relationship in particular, it may be hard to face signs and symptoms because underneath we sense the implications of mania and depression. On the surface, it may appear easier to sweep things under the rug, but in reality, recognizing the signs is a much healthier way to go about the dating process. There's more of a chance that things will work out for the best.

Profiling for Emotionally Blocked Men and the Obsessive Personality

HAVE YOU SAID, "I like you" or "I really enjoy being with you," to a man and gotten a look that is a bit strained, indicating that there are emotions stuck inside that he simply can't express?

This reaction is different from that of someone who isn't interested in you. He appears indifferent or disapproving of your expression of emotion. It's not due to garden variety commitmentphobia either. This is more severe.

It's as if his feelings—all of his feelings—and his ability to express them are completely blocked. Like or love aren't the only sentiments that he has trouble expressing. There are a whole range of emotions that don't see the light of day. Joy, tenderness, anger, hate, disappointment, and hurt are a few that he hides from women, the world, and, perhaps most frustratingly, himself!

Why would a man not allow his emotions to rise to the surface for himself and others to see? Why would he deprive himself of *feeling* all that there is to feel? In one word—fear.

When someone is afraid, he often attempts to gain control and to overpower the cause of the fear before it overpowers him. The obsessive personality believes that everything must be kept controlled—order, fastidiousness, and discipline will keep chaos at bay.

It's important not to confuse the obsessive personality with obsessive-compulsive disorder discussed among the anxiety disorders in Chapter 11. Obsessive-compulsive disorder involves specific obsessive thoughts and compulsive actions, whereas the obsessive personality is prone to control, rigidity, and perfectionism.

It's also important to make a distinction between the obsessive personality and the paranoid personality discussed in Chapter 9, because control is a major factor in both. The difference is that the obsessive man wants to control both inner and outer chaos through order and structure, whereas the paranoid man wants to dominate a world he presumes is out to get him. Thus it seems that obsessive men have more of a focus on *self*-control than paranoid men do. Remember, a chief fear for the obsessive is what he perceives as the emotional chaos within.

A Man Blanketed in Obsessiveness

THE OBSESSIVE PERSONALITY (termed "anal" by Freud) is another characterization that appears in literature. Scrooge in Charles Dickens's *A Christmas Carol*, with his rigid, miserly, and emotionally blocked ways, is an excellent example.

While Scrooge might not be your idea of a hot date, the reality is that Scrooge-like characters don't always present themselves in such a scruffy, grumpy package. You could come across a cute doctor, lawyer, or engineer who has learned to conceal some of his worst anal behaviors from plain view. As a matter of fact, in these professions and others, obsessive attention to detail and overorganization could (but not always) actually advance the person's position.

MONET DOESN'T GO WITH THE COUCH!

If you were offered a priceless Monet painting, you probably would not turn it down. Well, the obsessive personality might . . . if it didn't go with the colors in his couch! While it seems shortsighted and petty to turn down a masterpiece because it doesn't match the couch, believe it or not, this type of behavior happens. Think of the Monet painting as a relationship. An obsessive man is more likely to reject a special relationship when it doesn't meet his endless and outrageous standards, because every one of his picky demands is given equal weight with what others would consider more profound aspects of the relationship. For example, the fact that a woman has a messy desk (which he detests) is given equal weight with the fact that deep inside he looks forward to seeing her before every date (which he likes). In essence, her desk can cancel out his attraction.

This guy can't see the forest for the trees. It's hard for him to stand back and look at the beauty of the Monet painting as a whole and realize its intrinsic value beyond its color scheme. He is unwilling to accept any part of the painting that does not match his perceived need for it.

A PERFECT WORLD

The obsessive guy is a perfectionist. In his world, *everything* should be seamless and just so. That is likely to include you!

Being in a relationship with this guy might make you feel like you never quite measure up, no matter how hard you try. There's always something that you're doing wrong, according to him. Maybe the dishes aren't clean enough, maybe your body isn't thin enough, maybe you don't work at your job hard enough, or maybe your values aren't firm enough.

Research has shown that perfectionism is "associated with significant levels of impairment and distress not only for perfectionists but for their family members as well."[1] With a bunch of "shoulds" and "oughts" continuously landing on you, how do you think you would feel? Criticized? Defensive? Resentful?

Ironically, in the perfect world that the obsessive personality is trying to set up for himself, things can often be left quite disheveled and undone. Sometimes the perfectionist holds on to such excessively high standards that even he himself can't begin to meet them. He may procrastinate, taking forever to begin or end a project because he can't get it "just perfect."

DECISIONS AND COMMITMENT

Obsessive men dwell particularly over making decisions and commitments.[2] The thought process goes something like this:

> *If I choose A over B, I may be making the wrong decision. What if B is really the right choice and A is the mistake? Then I'll have to live with A and forever be haunted by B. B will flood my mind for the rest of my natural life. But wait. What if I commit myself to B and it turns out that A was the right thing all along . . . ?*

This thought process can be applied to everything from a new stereo to your relationship.

Decisions and commitments, both sizable and trivial, pose landminelike conditions for the obsessive man because he's obsessed with whether or not he will get the perfect outcome.

The challenge here is that the problems with decision making may be compartmentalized, affecting some aspects of his life more than others. So you have to keep your eyes open. He may have an okay time resolving issues at work, yet in terms of deciding to make a commitment to you, he could waffle forever. On the other hand, he may be able to commit to you fairly readily, but not for the life of him decide what restaurant to go to for dinner that night.

As you can imagine, if he experiences this much agony over decision making and commitment, he tends to avoid decision making and commitment. Holly, a twenty-nine-year-old project manager, found this out with twenty-eight-year-old Colin, a bright doctoral candidate in engineering. The couple had what they both described as a really fantastic relationship, yet after about five months, Holly learned that Colin was interested in switching doctoral programs midway. He had actually put out applications to programs across the country as well as abroad.

It wouldn't have floored Holly quite as much if the move made sense academically and careerwise. However, prior to this revelation, Colin had expressed a great deal of satisfaction with the engineering program, and professors seemed impressed with his work at grad school gatherings.

When confronted by Holly, Colin's rationale was that he had thought for a while about experiencing a different atmosphere and decided this was the time. Holly mentioned that "the time" curiously coincided with "the time" that their relationship was taking a more serious turn. Colin vehemently denied that he was doing this to escape their relationship. Holly was never quite sure. The one thing she was sure about was that their relationship was *decidedly* over!

RIGIDITY

Ironically, although the decision-making process might be a rocky road for the obsessive man, once the decision is made, it's practically intractable. With this kind of personality, "No" means *"NO!"* for now and forever. Switching positions or acknowledging that error could have crept into the decision-making process is too messy a thought to bear. The gray areas of life cause him overwhelming anxiety.

This kind of inflexibility can manifest itself in different ways. It can be time-based, meaning that he pitches a fit at lateness. It can be plan-based, meaning that his hairs stand on end if the day doesn't go according to his schedule. It can be home-based, meaning that if things are out of order or rearranged in his living space, disaster will ensue. It can be you-based, meaning that if you don't fit into his life like a perfect puzzle piece—chaos!

WORKAHOLICS

The obsessive guy tends to be emotionally blocked, and intimacy is a huge problem for him. If he experiences a little itty-bitty feeling of caring or an ounce of passion, a whole Pandora's box could blow open, causing him overwhelming anxiety!

One of the best places to hide from intimate relationships is work. The regimen, formality, and structure of the work environment provide a great haven from the emotional closeness that deep romantic relationships require. Bottom line: You'll notice the obsessive personality escaping to work and working to an extreme.

KEEPING UP APPEARANCES

Projecting an air of respectability to the outside world can be of major importance to the obsessive personality.[3] He likes to be seen by others as responsible, moral, and duty oriented. What he *doesn't see* is that his idea of responsibility is really more akin to hyperconscientiousness. His expression of morality is often closer to harsh judgment, and his concept of duty is more like way-over-excessive dedication.

Obsessive Perfectionism in the Relationship

IT'S NOT FUN to feel coldly dissected, harshly evaluated, or endlessly critiqued. No one wants to leave a date, or a relationship, for that matter, feeling like she couldn't live up to a set of impossible standards. No one in his right mind would want to cause someone to feel that way.

Faith, a junior in college, was floored when her fun relationship with Keanon turned sour after he stated, "We really need to start focusing on the pitfalls of our relationship." And he meant *focus*. She received text messages about areas of concern for him in the relationship that needed to be "explored."

The issues that Keanon brought up included, but were not limited to, the fact that she didn't like water skiing and he did; the idea that if they ever had kids, she might be stricter than he; their different political orientation; her penchant for Chinese food, while he preferred Italian.

Faith didn't want to ignore these issues, but she believed that both the big and small should be hashed out. The problem was that she thought Keanon was spotlighting the bad stuff, while the good stuff receded into the background. She couldn't keep up. When Faith wanted to "explore" his critical attitude, he truly was sorry she felt hurt, but he really didn't *see* it and in the end rationalized it all away. Unfortunately, Faith left the relationship in not such a good mood about relationships in general.

An obsessive guy may seem to have it all together at first, but you soon discover that keeping to his standard keeps you on your toes. In the relationship you're likely to feel:

- pressured to maintain rigorous standards in all that he deems important, such as an impeccable-looking house and kids
- detailed to death
- a lack of any and all spontaneity
- the need to appear picture-perfect to the outside world
- a scarcity of unconditional love
- a deficit of emotional responsiveness
- ignored
- scrutinized
- less important than his to-do list

That said, a little self-awareness goes a long way. An obsessive personality is always going to be an obsessive personality; who we are fundamentally doesn't change. However, a man who finds the motivation may choose to take action toward improvement. Options such as individual or couples therapy can help to ameliorate the worst of the obsessive symptoms so that the best of the repressed him can come through.

Is He Gay, Married, Cheating, or Addicted?

GET YOUR NAGGING QUESTIONS ANSWERED!

THERE ARE SOME THINGS about a guy that you simply need to know. And until you do, you're likely to have a sick, unsettled feeling that keeps you awake at night. You need to understand how to stop the wondering so the problem solving can begin.

Have you ever been or are you currently concerned about any of the following:

- Is my boyfriend likely to cheat? Is he being unfaithful to me now?
- Is the single guy I'm dating actually single?
- Is the single guy I'm dating gay?
- Is he addicted to drugs or alcohol?
- Is he a gambling addict?

Is My Boyfriend Likely to Cheat? Is He Being Unfaithful to Me Now?

THE SHORT ANSWER to the cheating question is that if he has done it before (to you or others), he's likely to do it again. Past behavior often predicts future behavior. Whatever it was in his psyche that allowed him to cheat before probably didn't vanish. It's still lurking there. Even though time has passed, the urge may not have.

AM I THE ONLY ONE BEING EXCLUSIVE IN THIS RELATIONSHIP?

At first glance, the definition of infidelity or cheating may seem pretty concrete—when a person has sex with someone other than his or her "designated" partner. However, at second glance, the meaning of sex can get fuzzy. Is kissing someone else cheating? Is oral sex cheating? Most women would probably answer with a resounding "Yes!" But the key is, would he? Does the guy you're dating have the same definition of sex or infidelity as you?

It gets more complicated when you bring other nuances of cheating into the picture. If you've been seeing him for two months and he goes out to dinner with another woman, that could be considered cheating. And what about cybersex? For many, that is cheating.

Of course, there are all types of emotional infidelity ifs. If he tells his deepest, darkest secrets to a woman at the office, would you feel cheated on? If he talks to a woman in an Internet chat room about problems he's having, is that being unfaithful?

As you can see, the important thing about defining cheating is that you don't keep the definition to yourself. You need to talk to him about it, particularly if you haven't delineated the terms of the relationship. For example, it's not a good idea to assume exclusivity in a relationship. If you do, you may be the only one who's being exclusive.

Of course, nobody wants to push things. Even if you've been on several dates, you may not want to be the one bringing up the "exclusivity" talk. Leaving things undefined for a little while can't hurt . . . just don't let it go on to the point where you feel really uncomfortable.

Sex is a particular hot-button issue in terms of exclusivity. If you're sleeping with him, don't assume anything about whether or not he's being faithful to you. If you want a monogamous sexual relationship, discuss it with him before sleeping with him and lay the ground rules. Following are ways to bring up exclusivity:

- Are you seeing other people? I'd like to know so that we can both be on the same page.
- I'm not seeing anyone else and I'm not really interested in seeing anyone else. How do you feel?
- I decided to take my profile off Match.com (check for his reaction to this statement).
- I don't have sex with someone unless it's a monogamous relationship. Do you feel the same way or different?

POTENTIAL CHEATERS

Infidelity expert Shirley Glass typically talks about affairs within the context of marriage. However, I'll extrapolate some of her information and apply it to dating and boyfriend/girlfriend relationships. Perhaps one of her most fascinating discoveries is that affairs happen in both good and bad relationships. Even if the guy is satisfied with you and your relationship, it doesn't mean he won't cheat.[1]

Glass identifies both social and cultural contexts as big predictors for cheating. That means watch out if a lot of his coworkers are

two-timing or if his friends are having affairs. It could be conta-
gious. But is he gravitating toward permissive friends and career en-
vironments because he wants to behave this way, or is the social
context causing his behavior? Most likely, it's a little bit of both, but
the fact remains that he's still prone to cheating if he's surrounded
by it.

Don't ignore his family background and culture. It's important to
notice if he has grown up in an environment that condones unfaithful
activity. Did his father or mother have affairs? Have the women in his
family looked the other way generation after generation? There are
many social/ethnic groups in which a man taking a mistress is the
norm. It's up to you to determine if that's the right norm for you.

When profiling for cheating, you really want to dig into his attitudes about issues like fidelity and adultery—subtle digging, of
course, but digging nonetheless.

Tira, a thirty-five-year-old engineer who was on the sixth date
with Jay, a forty-two-year-old in the same field, had a gut instinct
that she needed to profile for cheating. When Jay began a conversation about his friends' marital problems, she delicately extended the
dialogue. Apparently, his friends had a baby, which caused a significant de-escalation of their sex life. Jay went on to say that they have
sex only once a month. His exact words were, "Once a month, that's
frickin' ridiculous! There's no way—no way—I'd never put up with
that. If a guy's not gonna get it right at home, then he's looking elsewhere, he's goin' elsewhere."

Jay clearly laid his attitude on the table. In his mind, if sex wasn't
often enough or satisfying enough, then cheating is justified. It's as
though he had constructed a cheating clause for a relationship. The
implications sent Tira's head spinning. She kept thinking, "What if
we have a baby together and I don't feel like having sex for a while,
would Jay then cheat?" and "If I wasn't into some position that he

wanted me to try, would Jay then cheat?" After brooding over about a hundred "Would Jay then cheat?" scenarios, Tira decided to lay down her own condition—"Good-bye!"

If you have a no-cheating-under-any-circumstances policy, then you want to profile for the same. You want a guy who chooses to work out problems rather than threatening to look elsewhere or constructing excuses for cheating. You want a guy who believes that infidelity is never an option.

Guys who think cheating is an option tend eventually to give it away in their conversations and attitudes. Be cautious about men who go to an extreme in separating sex and love. While it seems many men separate sex and love, the key here is the extreme. Is he the type of guy who could be in a loving relationship with you and justify an affair because it's "only sex"?

Many of you might be thinking that because of the attitudes and values they hold, ultraconservatives are less likely to cheat than ultraliberals. But according to the *Janus Report on Human Sexuality*, a comprehensive study on American sexual behavior, 23 percent of the ultraconservatives surveyed reported having extramarital affairs that were frequent or ongoing.[2] This is opposed to 16 percent of the ultraliberals who reported often or ongoing extramarital affairs.

It's possible that ultraconservatives view sex as more sinful or dirty and wouldn't want to do sinful or dirty things with a spouse they love and view as pure. In this way, they save the naughty stuff for the bad girls on the side. You may want to watch for this as well as overreaction to cheating. If a guy is too preachy or harps on the evils of infidelity in overabundance, he could be repressing a major urge to stray.

In any case, it's easy to see how attitudes and beliefs play into possible infidelity. Don't worry about profiling for cheating all at once. As you get to know him, you'll get to know his attitudes toward sex, faithfulness, and monogamy. If he tries to cover up at first, you can still learn the truth behind the fiction if you keep profiling. No one can hide his real attitudes toward these issues 100 percent of the time.

Are You Being Cheated on Now?

MANY WOMEN MAY BE TORN over discovering the truth and may overlook what would seem to be obvious clues. A woman who's profiling has her eyes wide open to revealing behavior on his part.

"Missing" Time

Unaccounted for or "missing" time is one of the biggest indicators of cheating. When you get the feeling that he seems to be disappearing at certain points of the day or week, that's not good.

No man should have to give a woman an itinerary of his whereabouts, and being overly and unreasonably suspicious is one method of driving a good man away. However, you do need to protect yourself while at the same time maintaining the middle ground between being played and being paranoid.

Boredom

The cheating man may appear bored with his job, friends, and hobbies, as well as bored by your relationship with him. You may get the sense that it is tedious for him to spend time together as a couple or as a family and that he would prefer engaging in impulsive, thrill-seeking activities . . . like having an affair.

Lying

Covering up an affair leads to a web of lies, some tiny and some big. If you start discovering seemingly unrelated lies here or there, look to see if there is a connection between them and if that connecting point is an affair.

Many times, men who lie about cheating are in the habit of lying in general. It isn't a stretch for someone who is used to lying as a way of life to deceive you about being monogamous.

A Shift in Attentiveness

A noticeable shift in the amount of attention that he gives to you is a warning sign, particularly when it comes to sexual attention. It's usually thought that a man who is cheating has less interest in sex with his partner, which can be the case. However, it's also true that having an affair could serve as an erotic spark for him, causing an increase in sexual attention toward his partner.

There's also the guilt factor. An ashamed man may frequently initiate sex with his partner, buy her flowers, and shower her with special treatment. On the flip side, many men who cheat become neglectful and indifferent. The key is a shift from the behavioral norm.

On a cautionary note, if you notice a dramatic shift in your partner's attention toward you, it's cause for concern. It could be a warning sign for cheating, but it also could be a warning sign for a host of physical issues, mental-health issues, and problems that are occurring in your relationship. Take the time to rule these things out before you home in on cheating as the sole cause for his behavior changes.

If you suspect the guy you're with is cheating, generally the best action is to confront him head-on.

In the book *Affairs*, Emily Brown advises that when you suspect cheating without concrete evidence, your confrontation should take the form of a statement such as, "I think you're having an affair."[3] His response requires elaboration and makes it harder for him to lie. Asking a closed question like, "Are you having an affair?" doesn't give you much to work with because all it requires is a yes or no answer.

Although it might seem an impossible task, Brown advises that you speak calmly as well as patiently wait for his answer. If you're calm, he can't shift the argument by accusing you of being hysterical. If you silently and patiently wait for his answer, he will feel compelled to say something. Don't let him put you on the defensive by asking you a bunch of questions like, "What are you talking about?" or "Why are you saying that?" Simply and calmly restate: "I think you're having an affair."

During this conversation, call on the objectivity and therapeutic techniques that you've practiced as part of the profiling process. Observe him and notice the gradations of emotion and behavior as he reacts to you. His nonverbal cues may be just as important as his verbal ones. Is he being evasive? Is he excessively defensive? Is he caught off guard? His response could go a number of ways.

He Could Admit to Cheating

A confession could shake your relationship to its core. You will feel it, both physically and mentally. Although you may have been almost sure, and prepared yourself for this moment, a revelation of infidelity puts you at the epicenter of an emotional quake.

You'll also find yourself faced with a host of decisions. Many women choose to end the relationship, but many others choose to stay. It's a very personal decision based on a variety of factors, such as his degree of remorse, his level of commitment to the relationship, his past pattern of behavior, and his willingness to alter present/future behavior, as well as your feelings for him.

In these situations, couples counseling can be extremely helpful. It provides a good opportunity to identify and deal with what both of you are feeling. Also, his willingness to participate or not will tell you a lot about how much he values your relationship.

He Could Deny Cheating and Be Lying

If he continues to lie to your face, he's not addressing the problem and he's probably not particularly remorseful.

In instances such as this, some people resort to hiring private investigators and go to other surveillance extremes to get satisfaction. However it's really, really unlikely that a fulfilling relationship is achievable under these circumstances. Are you willing to fight for a relationship that is overgrown with cheat and deceit?

He Could Deny Cheating and Be Telling the Truth

Potentially, you could feel relieved. You expressed what you were thinking, he addressed your concerns with plausible explanations, and you believe him. All signs point to the truth: He isn't cheating. The problem is that he may not feel as satisfied as you. He may be hurt, angry, and frustrated that you don't trust him. You must accept that this is a normal reaction and help him process these feelings by talking with him about them in a nonjudgmental way.

On the other hand, he could be telling the truth, but you're still left wondering. If this is the case, there are definitely trust issues that you need to address. It's possible that there's something you just don't trust in him and it's manifesting itself as doubt about his fidelity. Can you pinpoint where your misgivings about him are coming from? Is he treating you the way you want to be treated? Is there something lacking in your relationship?

As always, self-examination is critical. Think back to some of your past relationships and what role trust and distrust played in them. Ask yourself if jealousy has been a big part in many of your relationships or just this one. It's important to explore whether you have trust issues with men in general, as opposed to with this specific man.

Remember, blaming yourself and learning about yourself are two different mind-sets. Blaming yourself is destructive; learning about yourself is constructive.

Is the Single Guy I'm Dating Actually Single?

THE "IS HE AVAILABLE?" question is definitely related to the "Is he likely to cheat?" question. Because availability/marital status is a basic thing women profile for, it's important to single this out for discussion.

The obvious way to test for availability is to look at his ring finger and check for a wedding band. However, many men don't wear a ring and others may be in a committed relationship without wearing a ring, so there's no tried-and-true test. He could be separated or engaged, so you have to do a bit more work to discover his true status.

Hunky twenty-six-year-old waiter John admits that he sometimes takes off his ring when he goes out to clubs. "It's not that I want to cheat or anything. . . . I like the attention. What can I say? I'm a social guy. No girls want to talk to me with the ring on."

There are probably few women who would want to waste their evening on a guy like John. He often goes as far as soliciting a number and not calling the woman. Interestingly, though, if asked outright, John does tell women he's married.

People often feel more justified committing lies of omission rather than telling outright untruths. They find it easier to rationalize not including information rather than deliberately giving out misinformation. It's like a personal "Don't ask, don't tell" policy.

You can catch those lie-by-omission guys by simply asking and compelling them to tell. It's easy to ask things like:

- Are you seeing anybody?
- So you don't have a girlfriend . . . or a wife?
- Any attachments? Any significant others?
- So are you engaged or married?

These questions, believe it or not, catch a large percentage of the spoken-for men out there. You can save yourself massive amounts of trouble by merely asking.

A small percentage of men are going to lie to your face about their attachment status. Take heart in the fact that this is definitely not a common occurrence. However, if you find that most of the guys you meet tend to lie about being single, it's a good time to adjust the profile of men you're going for.

He's going to lie not only about his marital status but a host of other things as well. You can profile for this guy by catching inconsistencies and gaps in his stories and, in general, following the guidelines for uncovering lies detailed in Chapter 10, "The Everyday Sociopath and Lie Detecting."

Is the Single Guy I'm Dating Gay?

HAVE YOU EVER GONE on a date with a guy and wondered if he's gay? Homosexuality, bisexuality, and the new pop distinction, "metrosexuality" (a straight man with the stereotypical aesthetic sensibility of a gay man) are big issues on the dating scene.

In *The Janus Report on Human Sexuality*, it was found that 22 percent of men reported having at least one homosexual experience,[4] which is why it's important to profile for his sexual preferences and orientation as well as exploring the types of sexual experiences that you are comfortable with.

As society has become more open toward homosexuality, it's probably less likely that gay or bisexual men feel the need to attempt to live a straight life. Yet it still happens.

Thirty-three-year-old Lexy found herself really liking twenty-six-year-old Stewart, although his effeminate physical characteristics combined with some stereotypical preferences for fashion and the arts bothered her in terms of his boyfriend potential.

One minute she would have her mind made up: "Absolutely, he's absolutely straight! When he kissed me he seemed totally into it. And just because a guy is effeminate and artsy doesn't mean he's gay." (Of course, Lexy is right about this; it doesn't.)

Then, however, she would find herself leaning the other way. Stewart made it very clear that his family's beliefs as well as his own dictate that homosexuality is wrong and that anyone who chooses to engage in homosexual behavior is a wrongdoer. Could he be repressing something?

Because she wasn't sure, Lexy went out on a few more dates with Stewart. Once, she noticed him in a long double-take of a beautiful male model on TV. Stewart then noticed her noticing him and became visibly agitated. Lexy wanted to talk with him openly at that point but felt that she couldn't.

Lexy ended the relationship soon after that incident—actually, less because of the gay question and more because she felt too repressed and afraid to have open discussions with him about this and other subjects!

It can't be emphasized enough how important candid communication really is.

Is He Addicted to Drugs or Alcohol?

THE FOLLOWING IS THE American Society of Addiction Medicine's definition of alcoholism:

> *A primary, chronic disease with genetic, psychosocial, and environmental factors influencing its development and manifestations. The disease is often progressive and fatal. It is characterized by continuous or periodic:*
>
> *Impaired control over drinking*
>
> *Preoccupation with the drug alcohol*
>
> *Use of alcohol despite adverse consequences*
>
> *Distortions in thinking, most notably, denial*[5]

Many would agree that the markers characterizing alcoholism are similar to the markers characterizing abuse of other drugs. How does this definition relate to the man you're dating? Does he continue to use despite adverse consequences, such as financial, legal, social, or health problems? Does he refuse to look at the possibility that there might be a real problem? Is he constantly focused on when, where, and how he is going to use?

THE POTENTIAL FOR SUBSTANCE ADDICTION

While he may not fit this definition, there may be aspects of the way he drinks that make you think there could be a problem down the road. In this case, this next list of characteristics will help you pin down more accurately his potential for alcohol and drug problems.[6]

Be sure to think of these characteristics in terms of degree rather than as all-or-nothing.

IMPULSIVENESS. Those who have a penchant for spontaneity, wear emotions on their sleeves, and can be described as blunt about what's on their mind are at *increased* risk.

PLAYFULNESS. Those who like sports, games, a lot of socializing, and doing things "just for fun" are at *increased* risk.

EXHIBITIONISM. Those described as extroverts who will try anything once or are willing to do something just for the experience of doing it are at *increased* risk.

LIFE STRESSORS. Those who experience a lot of pressure in their lives from any number of things, including problems at work or family issues, are at *increased* risk.

SOME PSYCHOLOGICAL DISORDERS. Those with certain psychological disorders, including sociopathy and attention-deficit/hyperactivity disorder, are at *increased* risk.

BONDING. Those who have strong ties to family, community, school, or church are at *decreased* risk.

ANTI–EVEL KNIEVEL. Those who don't participate in "exciting" activities, particularly ones that involve physical danger, are at *decreased* risk.

Other personality traits of alcoholics/addicts include the following:[7]

- immaturity in interpersonal and/or sexual relationships
- perfectionism
- hostility
- inflexibility
- depression
- compulsiveness
- the feeling of alienation/loneliness
- confusion regarding sexual identity
- low self-esteem masked by self-importance
- bottled-up anger/inability to express anger appropriately

BINGE DRINKING

Because it happens periodically, a lot of people don't equate binge drinking with being addicted to alcohol. As you profile, it's important to make the connection between the two. Binge drinking can be a serious addiction with serious consequences.

Chances are, if you're dating someone in a fraternity, you have a man on your hands who is a binge drinker, since 73 percent of fraternity members binge drink.[8] The definition of binge drinking used here for men is five or more drinks consumed in a row at least one time in the last two weeks. "Occasional binge drinkers" drank that much once or twice in the preceding two weeks, whereas "frequent binge drinkers" drank like this three or more times in two weeks. Does this profile fit anyone you have dated or are dating? The likelihood is that many of you are answering yes.

IS HE ON SOMETHING NOW?

There are times when knowing if a guy is on something becomes an immediate concern. It's too risky to be driven by or be alone with a man who's whacked out.

Elana will never forget the first and last date she had with an endocrinologist. He had only one drink after dinner, but as he stood up, his eyes rolled up and his body nearly flopped to the ground. She thought that the drink must have reacted with something he was taking—prescribed or otherwise. Elana waited a little while for him to sober up and then called a friend to take her home.

If you find yourself interacting with a guy who can be characterized by any of the following, be concerned and watch out for yourself.

sedated	out of it	freakishly paranoid
high as a kite	agitated	in a stupor
confused	slurring	uncoordinated
bizarre	twitching	red eyed and weary
dilated	having tremors	

Some of you may be thinking, "What if I'm at a party and meet a really cute guy who's drunk or slightly high?" Slipping a phone number to a guy like this rarely works because the call-back rate of intoxicated men is infinitesimally low. If you're blown away by him, find a way to track him down so that you can interact with him when he's sober. Also, try to learn whether or not inebriation is a common state of being for him.

HIS PROBLEM WITH DRUGS OR ALCOHOL IS YOUR PROBLEM, TOO

The following quote is from an interview with a thirty-six-year-old crack addict from the book *Cocaine: An Unauthorised Biography* by Dominic Streatfield.

Fucking evil. It speeds up your heart, it speeds up your fucking mind. It alters your mind to the point of not wanting to eat, not wanting to drink anything, not wanting to take a bath, not wanting to sleep. All you want to do is get more, get more, get more. So that you don't give a fuck what you got to do to get more.[9]

Later, as the addict continues to light up, he adds how "ashamed" he is regarding the neglect of his family. This small excerpt speaks volumes. There's no room for anything else in his life other than his drug of choice. Where do you think a woman would be on this guy's priority list?

The dichotomy of Dr. Jekyll and Mr. Hyde provides a good metaphor for drug addiction. Actually, *The Strange Case of Dr. Jekyll and Mr. Hyde* was written in 1885, the year that the "new" drug, cocaine, surfaced in English medical papers.

Unfortunately for many women, the experience of going out with a gentlemanly Dr. Jekyll can quickly turn into a Hyde-like experience when alcohol or drugs are involved. Many stick with the guy, hoping and wishing Hyde will go away. But unless he's taking definitive actions to do so, there's not a chance. Even if he is taking steps toward recovery, it's still a hard, uncertain road—although not an impossible one. The type of drugs involved, as well as the degree of addiction, play a key role here.

Many women (and family members, for that matter) who are involved with addicts "find themselves submerging or sacrificing their needs almost entirely in an attempt to deal with or help the user."[10] It's important for you to see the physical and psychological risks you face if you hook up with an alcoholic or a drug abuser.

Riding shotgun with an impaired driver, suffering through domestic violence, or becoming the victim of sexual assault are just a few possible situations you could find yourself in with an addict. Not to mention would-be psychological ramifications such as stress and depression.

When dating someone who drinks heavily or is into drugs, it's also important to look at the physical and psychological implications for him in the long term. Drinking's deleterious effect on the liver is common knowledge, but you may not be as aware that chronic use can lead to weakened heart muscle, high blood pressure, and memory loss, among other things.[11]

Researchers are also becoming more aware of the effect drugs have on long-term psychological functioning. For example, a concern about the club drug Ecstasy is that it may permanently alter serotonin systems in the brain, possibly leading to depression and trouble with mental functioning comparable to early dementia.[12] It's important to recognize that involvement with an addicted man includes not only today's complications but a future of obstacles as well.

Is He a Gambling Addict?

GAMBLING IS NOW AN ultra-accessible industry in our culture. If you want to do a bit of recreational wagering, you don't have to look far or hard. And as long as it remains "recreational," fine, no worries. It's when the bet gets a life of its own that troubles emerge.

Timothy O'Brien, author of *Bad Bet*, makes a good distinction between two pathological forms of gambling: compulsive gambling versus problem gambling. Problem gamblers are "those who regularly wager beyond their means but aren't addicted"; compulsive gamblers are "those hooked on gambling just as other people are hooked on nicotine, heroin, or alcohol."[13]

Because gambling can take such a vicious hold on a person, analogies to drug addiction are common in the literature. Just look at this description of video poker: "In its power to captivate and hook the player, video poker is said to be the crack cocaine of gambling."[14]

There are good reasons for making this analogy. First, likening video poker to crack emphasizes the gravity of gambling addiction. It's not an issue that can be ignored in a relationship. Moreover, drug/alcohol addiction and gambling addiction share many aspects. The out-of-control behavior, the "family disintegration" and, interestingly, the gradual building of tolerance are common to both types of addiction.

As with any addiction, a man will minimize and deny the fact that there is any problem or compulsion. But because you're profiling, you'll have a much easier time getting to the truth.

Here's a good rule of thumb to follow when profiling a man who may have a gambling problem: If he sets aside a certain amount of money for betting that is reasonable and within his means and doesn't go beyond that when he loses, it's a good sign that he's simply a recreational gambler. Start shopping for the red flag if, after he loses, he practically begs, borrows, or steals more money to play with. Also get a good handle on the frequency of his gambling. Does he seem a little too eager to place the next bet?

Too Many Questions About a Man May Be an Answer

It's only by addressing these "nagging questions," that you can start moving toward answers. Even if the questions don't apply to someone you're dating now, you're definitely well-armed for the future.

If you're asking all of these questions, and then some, about one man in particular—i.e., Is he a gay, cheating, substance-abusing, gambling addict?—don't waste your time looking for too many answers. Just having to ask a question like that is red-flag enough!

If you find yourself in a situation in which you continuously have nagging questions about a man that either (A) don't get answered to your satisfaction, (B) get answered in a negative way, or (C) leave you with a million more questions, it's time to evaluate what exactly you're getting out of this relationship.

As doubt after doubt about a man rise from your intuition, up goes the probability that the relationship will sink.

Profiling Online and Speed Dating

DIFFERENT WAYS OF bringing people together are constantly being invented and reinvented. You can switch on your computer and have a date at the click of a mouse, or in one night you can get to know twenty-five guys, four minutes per guy, at a speed-dating event.

In the face of these dating methods and venues, profiling gives you a system that fits wonderfully with all the new ways we meet people today.

For online dating and speed dating, you should apply all the techniques in the previous chapters with vigor and then some.

Dating Online

THIRTY MILLION AMERICAN ADULTS say "they know someone who has been in a long-term relationship or married someone he or she met online."[1] If you choose to begin profiling online for love, some of these thirty million Americans may be talking about your long-term relationship or how you and your spouse met online! In any event, heavily armed with the profiling process, negotiating and exploring the cyberworld is guaranteed to be an enriching experience.

Internet dating sites are a little like a grocery store of men. Reading profiles is somewhat analogous to reading food labels. You can get an idea of what you're buying, but you don't know if you like it until you give it a try.

Before you search for specifics, browse the many online dating sites to get an idea of what you're hungry for. If you want a popular site with a huge selection, try Match.com. If you're interested in finding a guy who comes recommended by other women, try Great Boyfriends.com.

There are sites that speak to particular interests: DemocratSingles.com, RepublicanSingles.com, CatholicSingles.com, JDate.com for Jewish singles, or a host of other sites that cater to your particular political or religious affiliation.

If a man with money is your heart's desire, MillonaireMatch.com helps connect women with rich men. If you want a smart man or an Ivy Leaguer, explore sites like RightStuffDating.com.

The good news is that once you start clicking like crazy for men, you're likely to make a connection. The average woman in terms of looks has a 70 percent chance of getting a reply from the average man.[2] Tempting odds!

Before you log on and start clicking for love, read the next section, which arms you with some key profiling strategies for the Internet.

DON'T GET PLAYED ONLINE

"In comparison to off-line circumstances, finding an exciting romantic partner online is easier and involves lower cost and lower risk."[3] The Internet has played a significant role in democratizing dating. Before singles' sites emerged, dates went to those who had the time and money to invest in looking for people to date. Now it involves much less hassle.

Think about how many times you need to go out to clubs, bars, or parties to find a viable date. For Pat, age twenty-nine, it averages about seven times of going out to one date. However, after she turned to Yahoopersonals.com, she's found herself e-mailing four men at once and dating at least two each week. Pat says that it's still time-consuming, but more time is actually spent with men than looking for men with no results.

The upside of dating online is its ease for women. The downside is that it's easy for men to find dates as well! Not only that, but the low cost and low risk for men can also amount to no-loss breakups.

Many men get bored with the endless turnover of women online, yet some don't because for them, online dating is like being a kid in a candy store. There are more than a few men who are online solely so they can date as many women as possible, so if you're looking for a serious relationship, it's necessary to weed out these guys.

ONLINE PLAYERS LOVE having their faces on dating Web sites. They love it so much, in fact, that they have a hard time taking their profiles off even when they are dating one or more women. Typically, Nonplayer Guy slows down on checking the site after a couple of dates. Then after a reasonable amount of time, by either mutual agreement or smarts on his part, the profile comes down. Of course, you do need to walk the middle ground between player and stalker. A man who takes things too slowly or a man who takes things too fast can both equal trouble.

ONLINE PLAYERS MAY SEEM addicted to checking the site. On most dating sites, you can tell whether people have signed onto it within the last hour, the last day, or the last couple of weeks. A man who constantly checks on the other women who are e-mailing him may be a player—particularly if he checks the site right after seemingly good dates or phone conversations with you.

ONLINE PLAYERS ARE quick to repost their profiles at the drop of a hat. Forty-year-old Cortez noticed that after she had a fight with her supposedly monogamous boyfriend, he put his profile back on without telling her. She considered this a form of online cheating.

ONLINE PLAYERS MAY BE on multiple dating Web sites without telling you. So even though he's not checking the one you met him on, that doesn't mean he's not active on other sites. When it comes time to define your relationship, the best thing to do is ask if he has an active Web profile.

ONLINE PLAYERS AREN'T all that different from off-line players, so look for the typical signs that indicate he may not be right for you. Sporadic attention, such as a long time between e-mails, phone calls, or dates, is probably one of the biggest indications that a man isn't.

ONLINE, A PICTURE IS WORTH A THOUSAND WORDS

"If flirting in the real world consists of no-strings banter between two people who feel mutual attraction, online flirtation is its inverse—it happens in the presence of everything *but* physical attraction."[4] This lack of physical presence in the first, flirting stage of a relationship is a big deal. In some ways it can be liberating; in other ways it can turn into disappointment.

Just because his e-mails flow like champagne doesn't mean his conversation will. Just because you seem to have everything in common online doesn't mean you'll be dying to kiss him off-line.

When online chemistry doesn't translate to off-line chemistry, many women feel horrible and plunge into self-blame. Some may blame the lack of chemistry on their looks; others may chastise themselves for not liking this perfectly nice guy.

Through profiling, you can avoid some self-blame, because gaining objectivity can help you shed the blame and guilt. You need to realize that if there's no hope for chemistry, you would be doing both yourself and him a disservice by beating a dead horse.

If you're in profiling mode, you won't fall into a depression because one guy didn't work out. Online dating (as well as dating in general) is a numbers game. Think of all not-quite-right dates as entertainment as well as learning experiences. After all, profiling helps you gain insight into the subjective world of another human being.

The fact of the matter is that you can't accurately profile for physical chemistry in the absence of physical presence. The only thing you can do is go with the information you have and take your best shot.

You don't go into an online experience totally blind because a photo may be posted with his profile. The ideal is when he has several pictures posted for your viewing pleasure. However, when he does have several pictures posted, you may notice one bad photo along with maybe one or two pretty good ones. It's probably a good sign that he's willing to post a photo that isn't the most flattering, but it does leave you wondering what he really looks like.

Averaging the best and worst picture is likely to get you closest to the reality of his attractiveness. If he has only one picture posted, it's a bit more of a gamble, but better than none. Depending on how important looks are to you, you could request additional photos. It's also important to acknowledge that some people don't photograph well and are much more attractive in person.

Many people completely discount any profile without a photo. There is an upside and a downside to this. The downside of a photo-only policy is that some men (like some women) do not want to have their face displayed on Internet dating sites. Of course, the stigma has vanished, but some people are simply private or cautious. Usually if no photo is posted, once you correspond the guy will volunteer to send a photo to you.

The downside is that no photo makes him more anonymous, which can be cause for concern. Does he want anonymity because he's private or because he's hiding something (like a wife)? One survey showed that men who don't include a picture on their profile "misrepresent their availability" twice as much as men who post a picture. And because 19 percent of men said they were single or available when they weren't, it's important to better your odds any way you can.[5]

VIRTUAL WOLVES IN SHEEP'S CLOTHING

"The freedom to obscure or re-create aspects of the self online allows the exploration and expression of multiple aspects of human existence."[6] The online experience taps into everyone's fantasy of reinventing himself or herself with the ultimate makeover.

An online makeover takes only a cybersecond. It's important to see the advantages in this. Sometimes people feel more free to expose their true inner nature online—the person they believe it's difficult to be off-line. Moreover, without the pressure of face-to-face interaction, exchanging e-mails can be more conducive to witty dialogue and scintillating conversation.

The more obvious disadvantage is that there are a lot of unhealthy men out there trying to hold it together just so they can look good to women. Most of them may not mean any harm, but some might. These are the ones you want to be particularly careful to profile out.

When dating online, there's a protocol that smart women follow and never diverge from: The slower you go—the longer you take to get to know a man—the more chances you have to see the real him.

Getting to know a guy on the Internet should progress from e-mail to instant messaging (if you like, although not necessary), to you phoning him, to meeting at a public place.

The first step, e-mailing, should go back and forth a few times. If you choose to give him your personal e-mail address, have one set up specifically for the guys you meet on the Internet. Once you decide to move on to phone conversations, let him give you his number to call. When you do call, if you don't already have a private number, use *67 (or some service like it) so your number won't appear on his caller ID.

Essentially you want him to reveal more information to you than you do to him. Perhaps this doesn't seem fair? While this might not seem open or fair, it's definitely better to be safe than fair in this instance. Besides, good guys realize that women need to be extra careful about meeting strangers. It's even considered a breach of netiquette to push a woman into giving her telephone number or meeting in person.[7]

If you decide to rendezvous with him face-to-face, make it a public place that's familiar and comfortable to you but not one of your favorite hangouts. You don't want to integrate this guy into your life yet. He's still a stranger, and you don't need him to know your hangouts and where he can easily find out information about you. By choosing a place that is somewhat familiar, a quick and easy "getaway" is possible if need be.

Throughout the entire process, from e-mail to meet-ups, keep track of the personal facts you divulge to him. The more you communicate to him, the easier it becomes to track down who you are. E-mails are the most controlled because you have the advantage of thinking them out before sending them. With instant messaging and phone conversations, a lot can be revealed quickly. It's important to use this to your advantage rather than disadvantage.

So what are you profiling for in each of these different levels of communication with him? You want to know if he's who he says he is. Finding out if he works where he says and holds the position he claims to have is a big part of this. A phone call to his place of employment goes a long way toward establishing the veracity of the information he has given you. Search engines like Google can also help you to find out information about him.

More generally, review the characteristics of rapists, stalkers, and liars presented in Chapters 4, 9, and 10. If he latches on to you too quickly, if he is sexually inappropriate in his communication with you, if you start noticing inconsistencies, such as a man who claims to be a doctor sending third-grade-level e-mails, beware.

The point is not to scare you out of your wits so that you never want to date online again. On the contrary, awareness empowers you in the process. As long as you profile and take the proper precautions, there's no reason for an anxiety attack. If a red flag is raised, don't ignore it. Take action and take care of yourself.

Speed Dating

SPEED DATING BRINGS you face-to-face with twenty-five to thirty men in one evening. Think about how long it would take you in everyday life to encounter and have conversations with this many new men!

The real beauty of it is that the encounters are boiled down to three or four minutes each. Who hasn't lamented over the blind date with one guy that wasted four hours of her precious time? Here there's no time wasted.

Still, you don't want to sacrifice accuracy for speed. Because you have such a short amount of time with each man, it's important to go in with a strategy. You can fine-tune your profiling for the speed of the situation.

FREE-FLOWING DIALOGUE OR STRUCTURED INTERVIEW?

During her second speed dating event, Jamica held hard-and-fast to the list that she created. The list was a set of about thirteen yes or no questions that she verbally went through with each man. Included were things like:

- Do you smoke?
- Do you have children?
- Do you want children?
- Are you divorced?

As you can imagine, there was a lot of debate among the men that night about her "technique." In an informal discussion with them later on, it turned out that some of the men were offended and felt like they were on the firing line. The majority of the men, however, didn't like it but weren't offended either. Of course, there was the minority who thought her technique was a good idea. One of these guys, after happily answering the questions, turned the tables and asked for her responses to the same questions, which was more than fine with Jamica.

One problem with this technique is that it seems overly businesslike and stilted. Also, because you're causing the men to conform to *your* set of questions, you might not be learning as much about them as you think. Oftentimes, the best way to learn about people is to create an environment in which they are free to express themselves.

For profiling purposes, it's best to modify Jamica's technique. Have two or three conversation points in your arsenal that will elicit the type of information you want. That way, you'll have some structure without sacrificing free-flowing dialogue. Also, if you want to get more out of him than "yes" or "no," come up with some open questions that require a more detailed response (see Chapter 2, "Getting into His Head and into His Heart").

Finding out what they do for a living is a good beginning. Some might argue that it's superficial to ask about work right off the bat, but the question is important. Because work is a big chunk of our day-to-day lives, employment can reveal a lot. For instance, it tells you their socioeconomic status pretty quickly. It can also give you an idea of their strengths, motivations, desires, and goals. By the way they talk about their jobs, you can find out how much they enjoy or despise work, which is a handy thing to know.

Perhaps the two most popular questions at speed dating events are, "What do you do for fun?" and "Are you having fun?" Although not necessarily bad questions, after you've heard them over and over, they can wear on you as well as the men at the event.

Profiling can help you break from the pack. You can distinguish yourself by using unique perceptions about him and the evening to create sparkling dialogue.

Instead of being the eighth woman to ask him, "Are you having fun?" profile the event and share some of your observations with him. For example, maybe you notice that people seem to be having a good time at this thing. One of your comments could be, "Everybody here seems like they're really energized and having fun. What do you think?" This way, you give an interesting opinion as well as elicit more interesting banter from him.

It's always a good idea to garner pertinent conversational cues from the guy and run with those. If you see him light up about a topic, pursue it. Even if he seems like he could get worked up about a topic in a negative way, pursue it. You're tweaking his passions—both positive and negative. Good information about him can come from that in a very short time span, which is key in speed dating.

MULTIPLE-MEN DELIRIUM

Monica declined an invitation to go with her friends to a speed-dating event because, as she put it, "I would mark 'yes' to everybody there. They'll all seem nice."

On the other extreme is Diana, who's lucky if she comes out with one "yes" all night. Her theory is that she can sense chemistry instantly, so why waste time if it's not there.

In terms of profiling, a middle-ground approach is most effective. If you're selecting zero to one person whom you would like to get to know further, it may be an indication that the profile you're looking for is a bit too black and white. Remember from Chapter 3, "Sketch His Profile," that you want to selectively profile as well as randomly profile.

Also, because of the way speed dating usually works, the more you choose, the more likely you are to get chosen. At the end, organizers tell you how many mutual matches you had, meaning the number of men whom you marked "yes" and who also marked "yes" for you. Then they tell you how many missed opportunities you had, meaning how many men chose you without you choosing them.

There is a tendency at about the tenth or fifteenth guy to start getting tired and confused. Beware, because this multiple-men delirium can cause a cavalier attitude to set in. Before you know it, a glance down at your check sheet will reveal that you marked "yes" to the guy with bloodshot eyes who punctuated every comment with a snort.

Speed dating is essentially a marathon combined with short sprints. Treat it as such. Many people head for the bar as soon as they walk into an event, which is understandable given the perception that alcohol is a social lubricant. However, everyone is aware of beer goggles and the haze of misjudgment that can come from one too many. For some good profiling, take it easy on the drinks during the speed-dating marathon!

Instead of an overload of alcohol as a crutch, try going with a friend or two to decrease your nervousness, or try seeking support and information from the other women there. Bonding often occurs in the women's restrooms during break time at these events, along with talk about the different men. It goes without saying that being careful of what you say is a must. At speed-dating events, your support is also your competition.

PROFILING BY ELIMINATION

Because you're going to be making quick judgments, it's important to profile by elimination. That means if bad things jump out at you about a guy, use them as criteria for a cut.

At one speed-dating event, Christa found herself sitting across from a guy who was flat-out wired. This wasn't a simple case of nerves, he seemed manic or in some kind of drug-induced state.

Other things that might give you pause and cause you to mentally say, "Next!" are:

- Men who manage to be bitter about their former significant other in a time span of four minutes.
- Men who seem pushy.
- Men who make inappropriate sexual innuendos (you don't have to sit there and take anything inappropriate—walk away and report him if necessary).
- Men who seem to have odd expression. Ask yourself if his level of emotion fits the situation. Nervousness and anxiety are a given, but do their emotions seem out of whack otherwise?
- Men who are too self-absorbed and do not demonstrate an interest in knowing about you.
- Men who are too slick.

- Men who have made a career out of speed dating.
- Men who creep you out at a gut level for no tangible reason!

Once you rule out the bad, you can concentrate on the good—chemistry, sweetness, intelligence, and so on.

Both speed dating and online dating are psychological adventures, so sit back and enjoy the ride. And remember, you'll wind up with some great stories and perhaps a wonderful man to date!

How Do I Know
When It's Love?

EVERYONE KNOWS THE SIGNS OF LOVE—you can't eat, you can't sleep, your concentration is out the window, he's on your mind every second of the day. Is this really a sign of being in love? Is he the one you've been searching for? Let's profile for love!

You "Just Know"?

CONVENTIONAL WISDOM SAYS that when it's real, you "just know." For some people, this may be the case. We've all heard stories of women who have gone out on a first date and said, "I'm going to marry that man someday," and they happily do. Others are not quite as definitive but have an intuition along the same lines. They may describe the feeling of "knowing that it's right deep down inside" or "sensing that this is it."

Then again, there are also the stories of uncertainty, confusion, and ambiguity, as well as the crash-and-burn of what seemed like true love.

Crashing and burning is a terrible feeling. You're left standing alone, stunned, wondering what just happened, and asking yourself if it was really love. This scenario is played out in the media as enraptured high-profile couples live out their love publicly one minute and announce their separation the next. Sadly, the thought that "it's right deep down inside" seems to have tricked them, and certainty about love turns into certainly not.

A little uncertainty about love is not necessarily a bad thing. Not being 100 percent sure about a man forces you to examine your relationship with a keener eye. So don't get upset with yourself if you're not one of the women who "just know" immediately. On one hand, in assessing the relationship, you could be saving yourself heartache by recognizing a false positive. On the other, you could be enriching your relationship by allowing it to nurture and grow in a thoughtful way.

Not Your Everyday Love Triangle

ROBERT STERNBERG, A RESPECTED RESEARCHER in the field of psychology, has come up with a multidimensional model of what he thinks love is. He identifies love as a triangle that consists of passion, intimacy, and commitment.[1]

- *Passion* is the force behind romance and sex.
- *Intimacy* is composed of warmth, closeness, and feelings of attachment.
- *Commitment* is the evaluation that, "Yes, this is love and it needs to be sustained and preserved."

According to Sternberg, different combinations of these three triangle legs generate different kinds of love:

- No Passion + No Intimacy + No Commitment = No way! This isn't love.
- Just Intimacy = You're in like, but not in love.
- Just Passion = INFATUATION
- Just Commitment = You're in a love void because it's empty love.
- Passion + Intimacy = Romantic love
- Intimacy + Commitment = Companionate love
- Passion + Commitment = Fatuous love (an immature sort of love)
- Passion + Intimacy + Commitment = Consummate love!!

Consummate love, which is the love triangle in its complete form, yields the most fulfilling, rewarding type of love. When both partners experience passion, commitment, and intimacy, it is considered to be the ideal relationship. In the course of this ideal relationship, passion is most prominent in the beginning and then levels off. Commitment develops more slowly, as does intimacy, which peaks more gradually than passion.

How do some of your past relationships or your current relationship fit into this triangle? The following questions are designed to help you think matters through, particularly if you're in a relationship now and trying to determine if it's love.

- How does your partner show you passion, intimacy, and commitment? How do you show him?
- If one leg of the triangle is missing, how do you feel about it? Is the relationship fulfilling enough as it is, or do you feel like two dangling sticks in search of a full triangle?
- If you don't have the full triangle with your current partner, do you believe you can get there with him? What steps will it take?

- Are both of you committed to maintaining the love you share, or is it a one-sided commitment? If it's one-sided, do you foresee a change in the near future?
- How high is the comfort level between you and your partner?
- On a scale from 1 to 10, how attracted are you to your partner?
- Do you have a true and natural interest in who he is? Is he intent on really knowing and understanding who you are?
- How do you rate your feelings toward him on each of the three dimensions?

SA-TIS-FAC-TION!

If you're thinking about love, chances are you're also thinking about marriage or will be at some point. You want to be able to evaluate whether or not you and your partner are likely to have a happy future together. To do this, it's necessary to look at what constitutes a bad marriage versus a good one.

In one good marriage/bad marriage study, it was found that you couldn't distinguish happy couples from unhappy couples based on their marital dissatisfaction ratings.[2] The reason? Everyone—the happily marrieds as well as the nonhappily marrieds—was disgruntled and dissatisfied about some things in their relationships.

What set apart the happy marriages from the unhappy marriages was their satisfaction ratings. The contented couples described "close, affectionate, and often romantic relationships."[3] So while they still had complaints about each other, these positive thoughts and feelings acted as a buffer, keeping the marriage in the happy zone.

As you probably noticed, the words "close," "affectionate," and "romantic" correspond very much to the passion and intimacy in the triangular theory of love. And because the couples in the study are married, it's implicit that they made a commitment to maintain their love, which is the third leg of the triangle. This supports the importance of having your triangle in shape. It seems like most of the happy couples were edging toward or altogether in "consummate" love, composed of passion, intimacy, and commitment. Not to mention satisfied!

So what about you? Are you getting any satisfaction? If you're getting a lot of it, this could be a good sign for the relationship. Satisfaction is the ultimate shock absorber for all of the annoyances, grudges, and complaints that are inevitable elements of human interaction. On the flip side, if you're low on satisfaction and high on dissatisfaction with him, that's a warning sign.

Take some time to jot down the things that satisfy you about your relationship and the things that dissatisfy you.

I FEEL SATISFIED WITH . . .   I CAN'T GET NO . . .

_____   _____

_____   _____

_____   _____

_____   _____

_____   _____

_____   _____

How do your lists weigh out? Remember, everyone has complaints and frustrations, so there needs to be some heavy-duty satisfactions to tip the scale. For example, maybe the guy is disorganized, which drives you crazy. Yet most every morning, waking up with him puts a smile on your face. That smile counts for a lot!

However, if your satisfied column lacks length and/or depth, while your dissatisfied column is off the page, it's time to ask yourself what you're getting out of this relationship. Is the relationship working for you? Do you think you can grow the "satisfieds" and decrease the "dissatisfieds" with effort?

Predicting Divorce

IN LOOKING AT what love is, one also has to look at what love is not. These are the factors that work against love, either to extinguish an existing love or to prevent love from taking hold in the first place. In the context of marriage, these are the factors that lead to divorce.

By learning what may predict divorce before you walk down the aisle, you can take the steps necessary for a positive future, which could mean working on problem areas with your partner or determining that he is not the right man for you.

One of the best-known and useful good marriage/bad marriage studies, which has ballooned into a wealth of knowledge over the last several years, was done by John Gottman and Robert Levenson.[4] During the course of their research, they have identified patterns of arguing that predict divorce with as much as 88 percent to 94 percent accuracy.[5]

Getting angry and arguing with your partner isn't necessarily the problem and is not a divorce predictor in and of itself. The key is *how* you both argue. During conflicts, when there is a pattern of more negativity coupled with less constructive, positive interaction, it's trouble.

This pattern of negativity during conflict comes in the form of four problem behaviors, "the four horsemen of the apocalypse":

(1) criticism, (2) contempt, (3) defensiveness, and (4) stonewalling.[6] If you've got one or more of these horsemen galloping into your relationship, heads-up because they are strong predictors of divorce.

CRITICISM

Criticism begins to creep into arguments when one or both of you attack the other's character. The specific thing you're arguing about gets lost in all-encompassing personality attacks.

For example, newlyweds Jan and Henry have an ongoing battle over wet towels left on the bed. It's gotten to the point that every time she plops one on the comforter and leaves it there, he calls her "lazy, just like your mother and sister." She then explodes into a diatribe on the flaws in his family as well as the faults in his character. Needless to say, what started out as an argument over a wet towel escalates to World War III by the time it's over.

Criticism such as this makes an argument mean. It creates stress and negative effect during the conflict, as well as hurt feelings and grudge holding afterward.

CONTEMPT

When contempt insidiously works its way into a couple's style of conflict, it can be emotionally abusive. Holding a contemptuous attitude toward a partner means being disrespectful and viewing him or her in a disdainful way.

Have you ever felt contempt coming from a man during an argument? If so, you may have noted palpable condescension in his eyes and in his stance. His words to you might have had a tone of ridicule and insult. He may have treated you like you were worthless, useless, and insignificant. It's not hard to see that contempt in all its manifestations is the antithesis of love.

DEFENSIVENESS

When individuals are on the defensive, they're in self-protective mode. The focus is on evading the oncoming attack at all costs. So rather than concentrating on the problem at hand and working toward a solution, energy is spent on shifting blame, justifying actions, and denying responsibility. When two people have been in a defensive argument, they tend to feel hurt and believe that they have not been heard or understood.

In this example, Alisha is being defensive with Sumner:

Sumner: *It's important for me to be at this dinner party thing on time tomorrow. We need to leave at exactly 7:00. That doesn't mean 7:15 or 7:30, Alisha.*

Alisha: *You're implying that I don't know what 7:00 means. [Here her voice goes up in volume.] I know what 7:00 means.*

Sumner: *Look, I'm just saying that this is important to me, and I want to be on time.*

Alisha: *I don't like your accusatory tone about my punctuality . . . and if you feel that way about it, you can go yourself!*

Instead of picking up on Sumner's anxiety about his big-deal dinner party, Alisha chose to get defensive about what she knows is her habitual lateness. The argument could have been defused by speaking to his feelings with a statement like, "I see this is really important to you; count on me being on time." If she didn't like his tone of voice, she could have added, "I'll be on time so don't worry, but the tone you're taking with me is making me angry."

STONEWALLING

Watch out, ladies, because stonewalling is a major tactic for the men, although we're not immune to it either. Stonewalling blocks communication, and with stonewalling comes avoidance and deadly, awkward silence.

A partner may stonewall through any number of methods. Staring at the TV during an argument is one of the most popular. A person may simply walk out during a fight in an attempt at evasion. Then there are those who refuse to hash out the conflict by saying, "I'm not going to discuss this with you" or "Leave me alone, I'm not listening."

A major premise of profiling is that people want to feel known and understood. When one person withdraws from the other and essentially refuses to hear what the other person is saying, that fundamental need doesn't get met. Besides which, nothing gets resolved when one or both partners retreat from the discussion.

Even though confronting these relationship killers may be difficult, it's important to honestly and straightforwardly examine the degree to which these horsemen participate in conflicts between you and your partner. Are you feeling the presence of all four or mainly one or two? Are the horsemen present to a mild, moderate, or severe degree? Which ones do you use? Which ones does he use? Are the horsemen there to stay, or is there hope for chasing them away?

Long-Lasting Love Means Arguing the "Right" Way

REMEMBER, IN LOOKING AT the relationship, you need to size up not only the four horsemen, which are escalators of conflict, but also the positive factors that resolve conflict. The following are some great fighting tactics that help keep anger levels low during the argument:[7]

- humor
- good-natured teasing
- communicating appreciation
- toning down complaints
- backing down from the hard line
- problem solving

To what extent do you and your partner use these positives when you are fighting? Can you increase these? If so, love has a good shot in this relationship as well as a long-lasting marriage!

Profiling your relationship for the presence of these positive behaviors together with the negative ones in an up-front, concrete way is essential. If you don't put it all out there with the attitude that you're ready to see it, you could be setting yourself up for a make-believe relationship. "In many relationships, people maintain a fantasy or illusion of love and connectedness while their behavioral manifestations and those of their partner are often devoid of affection, tenderness, or respect."[8] This is nowhere love. Profiling is a way out of nowhere to somewhere potentially great!

Love Him, Love Him Not

SO FAR WE'VE LOOKED at some of the things that make love what it is, including passion, intimacy, and commitment. We've also bit the bullet and examined some love busters, including criticism, contempt, defensiveness, and stonewalling.

Yet even with all the research, there is still that wonderfully unquantifiable aspect to love that partially has to do with love's subjectivity. Each and every person has his or her own unique experience of being in love. There may be commonalities such as the ones discussed, yet your love still belongs to you and only you. No one can presume to tell you what you're experiencing when you have these feelings for a man.

This brings us to one of the most personal "profiling methods" for determining whether or not it's love. Sit back, close your eyes, and bring to mind one or more people you have really and truly loved in your life. The important thing is not to limit yourself to romantic kinds of love. Think of love you have had for family members such as parents, grandparents, and siblings, as well as close friends and mentors.

Conjure up the impressions these special people made on you, the sensations they evoked in you, and the thoughts and feelings they left with you. You may find some things hard to put into words, and that's okay. You don't need to. You don't need to have words to know whether or not the man in your life evokes these same kinds of emotions and ways of thinking in you. Does this man make you feel love like you've felt before?

Take Amber, who had a strong, loving bond with her favorite aunt. As far back as Amber can remember, she recalls the enjoyment she got from making her aunt smile and laugh. To this day, Amber takes pleasure in "lighting up" her aunt's face by saying or doing silly things. Amber notices that with her boyfriend of about a year, she gets the same unique joy when she's able to "light his face up." It's the closest she's ever come to the feeling that she gets with her aunt.

Obviously, in this comparison as well as the ones you're developing, the romantic, passionate part of love is being set aside for the moment. When romance is introduced it does change things. Feelings of sexual attraction as part of love add an intensity and distinctive quality to the feelings you have for a romantic partner.

Yet when you really get into this exercise, you'll find that many of the people you love do bring out in you some of the same thoughts and feelings that your romantic partner brings out in you . . . if you love him.

Love *Isn't* Blind

TRUE, BEAUTIFUL, AND DEEP LOVE is not blind; it's quite perceptive. How real could love be—how much depth could it have—if a woman has no understanding of who her partner is but instead sees a fantasy man of her own creation?

When you love someone, you see him for the unique person he is. You understand and appreciate the richness of qualities that make him him. This man touches your heart and mind.

Profiling helps you get in touch with your heart and mind so that you become aware of who this man is and your intrinsic feelings about him. Do you feel generally happy about the fact that you're in a relationship with this person? There should be a special fondness for the man to whom you've chosen to devote your time and energy.

Many women are worried about overanalyzing every detail of their partner and relationship, but the reason they overanalyze is that they're going through the process in the wrong way. If you evaluate right, there's no need to dwell or overthink. Remember, profiling is smart and so is true love.

Notes

1. Empower Yourself Through Profiling

1. Associated Press, "Survey Reveals Real-Life Sex and the City," January 9, 2004.
2. U.S. Census Bureau, "Unmarried and Single Americans Week," *Facts for Features*, July 19, 2004, www.census.gov/Press-Release/www/releases/archives/facts_for_features_special_editions/002265.html.
3. Caroline Presno, interview with Alice Onady, M.D., 2003.
4. Gavin De Becker, *The Gift of Fear: Survival Signals That Protect Us from Violence* (New York: Little, Brown, 1997).

2. Getting into His Head and into His Heart

1. Carl Rodgers, *A Way of Being* (Boston: Houghton Mifflin, 1980).
2. Janet Moursund and Maureen C. Kenny, *The Process of Counseling and Therapy*, 4th ed. (Upper Saddle River, NJ: Prentice-Hall, 2002).
3. Bruce Rybarczyk and Albert Bellg, *Listening to Life Stories: A New Approach to Stress Intervention in Health Care* (New York: Springer, 1997).
4. Ibid.

3. Sketch His Profile

1. Viktor Frankl, *Man's Search for Meaning: An Introduction to Logotherapy*, trans. Ilse Lasch (Boston: Beacon Press, 1962).

4. Sexual Attraction, Chemistry, and Phero-moans

1. George Preti, Charles J. Wysocki, Kurt T. Barnhart, Steven J. Sondheimer, and James J. Leyden, "Male Auxiliary Extracts Contain Pheromones That Affect Pulsatile Secretion of Luteinizing Hormone and Mood in Women Recipients," *Biology of Reproduction* 68, no. 6 (2003): 2107–13.
2. Claus Wedekind, Thomas Seebeck, Florence Bettens, and Alexander J. Paepke, "MHC-Dependent Mate Preferences in Humans," *Proceedings of the Royal Society of London* 260 no. 1359 (1995): 245–49.
3. Rachael Combe, "Drugs and Your Love Life: Does What You Take Affect Who You Pick?" *Elle*, August 2003, p. 98.
4. Michelle Kodis, with David T. Moran and Deborah Houy, *Love Scents: How Your Natural Pheromones Influence Your Relationships, Your Moods, and Who You Love* (New York: Dutton, 1998).
5. Michael D. Lemonick, "The Chemistry of Desire: Everyone Knows What Lust Feels Like. Scientists Are Now Starting to Understand How It Happens," *Time*, January 19, 2004.
6. Leslie A. Zebrowitz, *Reading Faces: Window to the Soul?* (Boulder, CO: Westview Press, 1997).
7. Ian S. Penton-Voak and David I. Perrett, "Female Preference for Male Faces Changes Cyclically," *Evolution and Human Behavior* 21, no. 1 (2000): 39–48.
8. David M. Buss, *The evolution of Desire: Strategies of Human Mating*, rev. ed. (New York: Basic Books, 2003).
9. John T. Molloy, *Why Men Marry Some Women and Not Others* (New York: Time Warner, 2004).
10. Paula Hall, *Difficulty Reaching Orgasm*, 2006, www.bbc.co.uk.

5. The Dark Side of Sex: Profile and Protect Yourself

1. Ronet J. Bachman and Linda E. Saltzman, *Violence Against Women: Estimates from the Redesigned Survey*, Report no. NCJ-154348 (Washington, DC: U.S. Department of Justice, Bureau of Justice Statistics, August 1995).
2. Heather M. Gray and Vangie A. Foshee, "Adolescent Dating Violence: Differences Between One-Sided and Mutually Violent Profiles," *Journal of Interpersonal Violence* 12, no. 1 (1997): 126–41.
3. Andrea Parrot, *Coping with Date Rape and Acquaintance Rape* (New York: Rosen Publishing, 1995).
4. Ibid.
5. Thomas L. Jackson, ed., *Acquaintance Rape: Assessment, Treatment, & Prevention* (Sarasota, FL: Professional Resource Press, 1996).
6. Ibid.
7. Ibid.
8. Ibid.
9. Parrot, *Coping with Date Rape*.
10. Centers for Disease Control and Prevention, National Center for Injury Prevention and Control, "Dating Violence Fact Sheet," www.cdc.gov.
11. Jackson, *Acquaintance Rape*.
12. CDC, "Dating Violence Fact Sheet."
13. Merril D. Smith, ed., *Sex Without Consent: Rape and Sexual Coercion in America* (New York: New York University Press, 2001).
14. Scott Lindquist, *The Date Rape Prevention Book: The Essential Guide for Girls & Women* (Naperville, IL: Sourcebooks, Inc., 2000).

6. Commitment-Ready Men versus Commitment-Phobic Men: Learn How to Not Get Used!

1. John H. Harvey and Amy Wenzel, eds., *A Clinician's Guide to Maintaining and Enhancing Close Relationships* (Mahwah, NJ: Lawrence Erlbaum, 2002).

2. Barbara Dafoe Whitehead and David Popenoe, "Why Men Won't Commit: Exploring Young Men's Attitudes About Sex, Dating and Marriage," *The State of Our Unions*, National Marriage Project, Rutgers University, 2002.

3. Matthew D. Bramlett and William D. Mosher, "Cohabitation, Marriage, Divorce, and Remarriage in the United States," National Center for Health Statistics, *Vital and Health Statistics* 23, no. 22 (2002).

4. Ibid.

5. Patrick McDonagh, "Sex, Lives, and Commitment," *McGill Reporter*, April 8, 1999, http://ww2mcgill.ca/uro/rep/r3114/x3114.html.

6. Neil Chethik, *VoiceMale: What Husbands Really Think About Their Marriages, Their Wives, Sex, Housework, and Commitment* (New York: Simon and Schuster, 2006).

7. Bramlett and Mosher, "Cohabitation, Marriage, Divorce, and Remarriage."

8. Richard A. Mackey and Bernard A. O'Brien, *Lasting Marriages: Men and Women Growing Together* (Westport, CT: Praeger, 1995).

9. Aaron Ben-Ze'ev, *Love Online: Emotions on the Internet* (New York: Cambridge University Press, 2004).

10. Molloy, *Why Men Marry Some Women and Not Others*.

11. Ibid.

12. Chethik, *VoiceMale*.

13. "Girls Gone Wired," *Elle*, June, 2004, p. 99.

7. *Discovering Mr. Self-Actualized*

1. Abraham H. Maslow, *Toward a Psychology of Being*, 2nd ed. (New York: Van Nostrand Reinhold, 1968).

2. www.hbo.com/city/cast/character/aidan_shaw.shtml.

3. Allison Glock, "Nick Lachey: King of Pain," *RollingStone*, April 21, 2006, www.rollingstone.com.

4. Abraham H. Maslow, *The Farther Reaches of Human Nature* (New York: Viking, 1971).

5. Abraham H. Maslow, *Motivation and Personality*, 3rd ed. (New York: Harper, 1987).
6. Maslow, *Toward a Psychology of Being*.
7. Ibid.

8. Date with a Narcissist

1. Nathan Schwartz-Salant, *Narcissism and Character Transformation: The Psychology of Narcissistic Character Disorders* (Toronto: Inner City Books, 1982).
2. American Psychiatric Association, *Diagnostic and Statistical Manual of Mental Disorders*, 4th ed., text revision (Washington, DC: APA, 2000).
3. Schwartz-Salant, *Narcissism and Character Transformation*.
4. American Psychiatric Association, *Diagnostic and Statistical Manual*.
5. John G. Gunderson, Elsa Ronningstam, and Lauren E. Smith, "Narcissistic Personality Disorder," in *The DSM-IV Personality Disorders*, ed. W. John Livesley (New York: Guilford, 1995).
6. American Psychiatric Association, *Diagnostic and Statistical Manual*.
7. W. Keith Campbell and Craig A. Foster, "Narcissism and Commitment in Romantic Relationships: An Investment Model Analysis," *Personality and Social Psychology Bulletin* 28, no. 7 (2002): 484–495.

9. Passion, Power, and Paranoia

1. Fenton Bresler, *Napoleon III: A Life* (New York: Carroll & Graf, 1999).
2. Frances Mossiker, *Napoleon and Josephine: The Biography of a Marriage* (New York: Simon and Schuster, 1999).
3. Ibid.
4. Robert S. Robins and Jerrold M. Post, *Political Paranoia: The Psychopolitics of Hatred* (New Haven, CT: Yale University Press, 1997).
5. Ibid.
6. American Psychiatric Association. *The Diagnostic and Statistical Manual of Mental Disorders*, 3rd ed. rev. (Washington, DC: APA, 1987).

7. Robins and Post, *Political Paranoia*.

8. Michael H. Stone, *Abnormalities of Personality: Within and Beyond the Realm of Treatment* (New York: W. W. Norton, 1993).

9. Evan Stark and Ann Filtcraft, "Violence Among Intimates: An Epidemiological Review," in *Handbook of Family Violence*, ed. Vincent B. Van Hasselt, R. L. Morrison, Allen S. Bellack, and Michel Hersen (New York: Plenum, 1987).

10. Eve S. Buzawa and Carl G. Buzawa, *Domestic Violence: The Criminal Justice Response*, 3rd ed. (Thousand Oaks, CA: Sage Publications, 2003).

11. Lenore E. Walker, *The Battered Woman Syndrome* (New York: Springer, 1984).

12. Orit Kamir, *Every Breath You Take: Stalking Narratives and the Law* (Ann Arbor: University of Michigan Press, 2001).

13. De Becker, *Gift of fear*.

14. Steven J. Morewitz, *Stalking and Violence: New Patterns of Trauma and Obsession* (New York: Kluwer Academic/Plenum Publishers, 2002).

15. Robert L. Snow, *Stopping a Stalker: A Cop's Guide to Making the System Work for You* (New York: Plenum, 1998).

16. Morewitz, *Stalking and Violence*.

10. The Everyday Sociopath and Lie Detecting

1. The term "everyday sociopath" was inspired by the heading "Wanted: Everyday Psychopaths" in Robert C. Carson, James N. Butcher, and Susan Mineka, *Abnormal Psychology and Modern Life*, 11th ed. (Boston: Allyn and Bacon, 2000).

2. Theodore Millon and Roger Davis, *Personality Disorders in Modern Life* (New York: John Wiley, 2000).

3. Cathy S. Widom, "A Methodology for Studying Non-Institutionalized Psychopaths," in *Psychopathic Behaviour: Approaches to Research*, ed. Robert D. Hare and Daisy Schalling (New York: John Wiley, 1978).

4. W. John Livesley, *Practical Management of Personality Disorders* (New York: Guilford Press, 2003).

5. Theodore Millon, *Disorders of Personality: DSM-III: Axis II* (New York: John Wiley, 1981).

6. Ann Rule, *The Stranger Beside Me: Ted Bundy: The Classic Story of Seduction and Murder*, updated twentieth anniversary edition (New York: W. W. Norton, 2000).

7. Joe Navarro, "A Four-Domain Model for Detecting Deception: An Alternative Paradigm for Interviewing," *FBI Law Enforcement Bulletin* (June 2003), www.fbi.gov.

8. Leslie A. Zebrowitz, *Reading Faces: Window to the Soul?* (Boulder, CO: Westview Press, 1997).

9. Ibid.

10. Navarro, "A Four-Domain Model."

11. Joe Navarro and John R. Schafer, "Detecting Deception," *FBI Law Enforcement Bulletin* (July 2001), www.fbi.gov.

12. Ibid.

11. Is Your Guy Anxiety Ridden and Stressed Out?

1. Tracey E. Madden, Lisa F. Barrett, and Paula R. Pietromonaco, "Sex Differences in Anxiety and Depression: Empirical Evidence and Methodological Questions," in *Gender and Emotion: Social Psychological Perspectives*, ed. Agneta H. Fischer (New York: Cambridge University Press, 2000).

2. David H. Barlow, *Anxiety and Its Disorders: The Nature and Treatment of Anxiety and Panic*, 2nd ed. (New York: Guilford Press, 2002).

3. Robert C. Carson, James N. Butcher, and Susan Mineka, *Abnormal Psychology and Modern life*, 11th ed. (Boston: Allyn and Bacon, 2000).

4. Thomas H. Holmes and Richard H. Rahe, "The Social Readjustment Rating Scale," *Journal of Psychosomatic Research* 11, no. 2 (1967): 213–18.

5. Diana Sanders and Frank Wills, *Counseling for Anxiety Problems*, 2nd ed. (Thousand Oaks, CA: Sage Publications, 2003).

6. Bernadette H. Schell, *A Self-Diagnostic Approach to Understanding Organizational and Personal Stressors: The C-O-P-E Model for Stress Reduction* (Westport, CT: Quorum Books, 1997).

7. Ibid.

8. American Psychiatric Association, *Diagnostic and Statistical Manual*, 4th ed.

9. Eve B. Carlson, *Trauma Assessments: A Clinician's Guide* (New York: Guilford Press, 1997).

10. Ibid.

11. Richard K. James and Burl E. Gilliland, *Crisis Intervention Strategies*, 4th ed. (Belmont, CA: Wadsworth/Thomson Learning, 2001).

12. Lydia C. Jackson and Amy Wenzel, "Anxiety Disorders and Relationships: Implications for Etiology, Functionality, and Treatment, in Harvey and Wenzel, *A Clinician's Guide*, 2002.

13. Louis A. Schmidt and Jay Schulkin, eds. *Extreme Fear, Shyness, and Social Phobia: Origins, Biological Mechanisms, and Clinical Outcomes* (New York: Oxford University Press, 1999).

14. Samuel M. Turner, Deborah C. Beidel, and R. M. Townsley, "Social Phobia: Relationship to Shyness," *Behaviour Research and Therapy* 28 (1990): 497–505.

15. Ibid.

16. Aushalom Caspi, Glen H. Elder, Jr., and Daryl J. Bem, "Moving Away from the World: Life Course Patterns of Shy Children," *Developmental Psychology* 24 (1988): 824–31.

17. Stanley J. Rachman, "An Overview of Clinical and Research Issues in Obsessive-Compulsive Disorders," in *Obsessive-Compulsive Disorder: Psychological and Pharmacological Treatment*, ed. Matig Mavissakalian, Samuel M. Turner, and Larry Michelson (New York: Plenum Press, 1985).

18. Barlow, *Anxiety and Its Disorders*.

19. John R. White, *Overcoming Generalized Anxiety Disorder: A Relaxation, Cognitive Restructuring, and Exposure-Based Protocol for the Treatment of GAD* (Oakland, CA: New Harbinger Publications, 1999).

20. American Psychiatric Association, *Diagnostic and Statistical Manual*, 4th ed.

21. Jill H. Rathus and Gregory M. Asnis, "Panic Disorder Phenomenology and Differential Diagnosis," in *Panic Disorder: Clinical, Biological, and*

Treatment Aspects, ed. Gregory M. Asnis and Herman M. van Pragg (New York: John Wiley, 1995).

22. Michael H. Zal, *Panic Disorder: The Great Pretender* (New York: Insight Books, 1990).

23. Mentalhealthchannel, "Obsessive Compulsive Disorder (OCD)," 2006, www.mentalhealthchannel.net/ocd/.

12. Forecasting the Dark Days of Depression and High Pressure of Mania

1. Geo Stone, *Suicide and Attempted Suicide: Methods and Consequences* (New York: Carroll & Graf, 1999).

2. Elizabeth Wurtzel, *Prozac Nation: Young and Depressed in America* (New York: Riverhead Books, 1994).

3. Gary R. Brooks and Glenn E. Good, eds, *The New Handbook of Psychotherapy and Counseling with Men: A Comprehensive Guide to Settings, Problems, and Treatment Approaches*, Vol. 1 (San Francisco: Jossey-Bass, 2001).

4. American Psychiatric Association, *Diagnostic and Statistical Manual*, 4th ed.

5. John R. Lynch and Christopher Kilmartin, *The Pain Behind the Mask: Overcoming Masculine Depression* (Binghamton, NY: Haworth Press, 1999).

6. Sam V. Cochran and Fredric E. Rabinowitz, *Men and Depression: Clinical and Empirical Perspectives* (San Diego, CA: Academic Press, 2000).

7. Ibid.

8. Lynch and Kilmartin, *Pain Behind the Mask*.

9. Cochran and Rabinowitz, *Men and Depression*.

10. Steven R. H. Beach and K. Daniel O'Leary, "Dysphoria and Marital Discord: Are Dysphoric Individuals at Risk for Marital Maladjustment?" *Journal of Marital and Family Therapy* 19 (1993): 355–68.

11. Thomas E. Joiner and James C. Coyne, eds., *The Interactional Nature of Depression: Advances in Interpersonal Approaches* (Washington, DC: American Psychological Association, 1999).

12. David J. Miklowitz, *The Bipolar Disorder Survival Guide: What You and Your Family Need to Know* (New York: Guilford Press, 2002).

13. Peter C. Whybrow, *A Mood Apart: Depression, Mania, and Other Afflictions of the Self* (New York: Basic Books, 1997).

14. American Psychiatric Association, *Diagnostic and Statistical Manual*, 4th ed.

15. Ibid.

16. Mario Maj, Hagop S. Akiskal, Juan J. López-Ibor, and Norman Sartorius, eds., *Bipolar Disorder*, Vol. 5 (New York: John Wiley, 2000).

13. Profiling for Emotionally Blocked Men and the Obsessive Personality

1. Gordon L. Flett and Paul L. Hewitt, eds., *Perfectionism: Theory, Research, and Treatment* (Washington, DC: American Psychological Association, 2002).

2. Allan E. Mallinger and Jeannette De Wyze, *Too Perfect: When Being in Control Gets out of Control* (New York: Clarkson Potter, 1992).

3. Bruce Pfohl and Nancy Blum, "Obsessive-Compulsive Personality Disorder," in *The DSM-IV Personality Disorders*, ed. W. John Livesley (New York: Guilford Press, 1995).

14. Is He Gay, Married, Cheating, or Addicted? Get Your Nagging Questions Answered!

1. Shirley Glass and Hara E. Marano, "Shattered Vows," *Psychology Today*, July–August 1998, www.psychologytoday.com.

2. Samuel S. Janus and Cynthia L. Janus, *The Janus Report on Sexual Behavior* (New York: John Wiley, 1993).

3. Emily M. Brown, *Affairs: A Guide to Working Through the Repercussions of Infidelity* (San Francisco: Jossey-Bass, 1999).

4. Janus and Janus, *The Janus Report*.

5. American Society of Addiction Medicine, Public Policy Statement on

the Definition of Alcoholism (adopted September 1976, revised February 1990), www.ASAM.org.

6. Jean Kinney, *Loosening the Grip: A Handbook of Alcohol Information*, 7th ed. (New York: McGraw-Hill, 2003).

7. Richard Fields, *Drugs in Perspective: A Personalized Look at Substance Use and Abuse*, 3rd ed. (Boston: WCB/McGraw-Hill, 1998).

8. Henry Wechsler and Bernice Wuethrich, *Dying to Drink: Confronting Binge Drinking on College Campuses* (New York: Rodale, 2002).

9. Dominic Streatfield, *Cocaine: An Unauthorised Biography* (New York: St. Martin's Press, 2001).

10. Bill Reading and Michael Jacobs, *Addiction: Questions and Answers for Counselors and Therapists* (Philadelphia: Whurr Publishers, 2003).

11. Julie A. Hogan, Kristen R. Gabrielsen, Nora Luna, and Denise Grothaus, *Substance Abuse Prevention: The Intersection of Science and Practice* (Boston: Pearson Education, 2003).

12. Richard Hammersley, Furzana Khan, and Jason Ditton, *Ecstasy and the Rise of the Chemical Generation* (New York: Routledge, 2002).

13. Timothy L. O'Brien, *Bad Bet: The Inside Story of the Glamour, Glitz, and Danger of America's Gambling Industry* (New York: Random House, 1998).

14. Katherine V. Wormer and Diane R. Davis, *Addiction Treatment: A Strengths Perspective* (Pacific Grove: CA: Brooks/Cole, 2003).

15. Profiling Online and Speed Dating

1. Mary Madden and Amanda Lenhart. "Online Dating: Americans Who Are Seeking Romance Use the Internet to Help Them in Their Search, but There is Still Widespread Public Concern About the Safety of Online Dating" (Washington, D.C.: Pew Internet and American Life Project, 2006).

2. Guenter Hitsch, Ali Hortacsu, and Dan Aricly, "What Makes You Click? An Empirical Analysis of Online Dating," paper presented at the University of California, Santa Cruz, Economics Department Seminar, 2004, http://repositories.cdlib.org/ucsc_econ_seminar/winter2005/3.

3. Ben-Ze'ev, *Love Online*.

4. Egan, "Love in the Time of No Time."

5. Jane Weaver, *Personals, Sex Sites Changing the Rules of Love: Women are Reaping Big Rewards from Online Dating*, May 19, 2004, www.msnbc. msn.com/id/4917480.

6. J. Gackenbach, ed., *Psychology and the Internet: Intrapersonal, Interpersonal, and Transpersonal Implications* (San Diego: Academic Press, 1998).

7. Ben-Ze'ev, *Love Online*.

16. How Do I Know When It's Love?

1. Robert J. Sternberg, *The Triangle of Love* (New York: Basic Books, 1988).

2. Arlene Skolnick, "Grounds for Marriage: Reflections and Research on an Institution in Transition," in *Inside the American Couple: New Thinking/New Challenges*, ed. Marilyn Yalom and Laura L. Carstensen (Berkeley: University of California Press, 2002).

3. Ibid.

4. John M. Gottman and Robert W. Levenson, "Marital Processes Predictive of Later Dissolution: Behavior, Physiology, and Health," *Journal of Personality and Social Psychology* 63, no. 2 (1992): 221–33.

5. John M. Gottman and Sybil Carrere, "Welcome to the Love Lab," *Psychology Today*, September 2000, www.psychologytoday.com/articles/pto-20000901-000033.html.

6. John M. Gottman, *Why Marriages Succeed or Fail: And How You Can Make Yours Last* (New York: Fireside, 1994).

7. Gottman and Carrere, "Welcome to the Love Lab."

8. Robert W. Firestone and Joyce Catlett, *Fear of Intimacy* (Washington, DC: American Psychological Association, 1999).

Index

Machiavellian types, 147
major histocompatibility complex
(MHC), 47
male pheromones, 46
mania. *See* depression and mania
Maslow, Abraham, 92–94, 95, 101–3
men (commitment-ready vs.
commitment phobic), 72–91
casual sex, 82–83
change and compromise, avoidance
of, 84–85
commitment, shapes and sizes of,
76–77
commitment, thoughts of, 80–81
commitment facts, 87–88
commitment-ready vs. commitment
phobic, 88–90
emotional use and abuse, 74–76
honorable intentions, 78–79
live-in girlfriend, 83–84
marriage, 85–87
psychological attachment, 79–80
stay or bolt, 90–91
ten top reasons men won't commit,
81–82
use me up, 73–74
Mr. Self-Actualized, 92–116
model man for model woman, 105
needs, taking stock of, 103–4
true ethical man vs. petty-anal guy,
99
what he needs, 101–3
Mr. Self-Actualized (top ten
characteristics), 93–101
creative, 95
curious, 97
ethical, 98
funny, 100–101
humble, 99

independent, 96–97
open, 99
"peak experience," ability to enjoy,
101
perceptive, 95
warm, 97–98

Napoleon and Josephine, 117–18
narcissist (dating), 106–16
characteristics, 107–8
cluelessness, 112
in love with love, 114–15
insensitivity, 113–14
matter of degree, 115–16
me, myself, and I, 108–9
mirror, mirror on the wall, 110
pathological envy, 112
trophy dating and flattery, 111
National Marriage Project, 81–84,
85–87
Nicholson, Jack, 54, 164
Nixon, Richard, 119

O'Brien, Timothy, 208–9
obsessive-compulsive tendencies,
164–65
obsessiveness, 184–89
decisions and commitment, 186–87
keeping up appearances, 188–89
outrageous standards, 185
perfectionism, 185–86
rigidity, 187–88
workaholics, 188
Onady, Dr. Alice, 7
online dating, 211–18
photos, 214 16
virtual wolves, 216–18
Open Range (film), 137
openness, self-actualized man and, 99

About the Author

CAROLINE PRESNO, ED.D., P.C.C., is a psychotherapist licensed by the state of Ohio in the practice of mental health counseling, as well as a doctor of education. Dr. Caroline has helped and entertained thousands of listeners and viewers through her radio and TV spots. Her profiling techniques have been honed through academic research, clinical experience, and her own always-exciting dates that led her to "The One"!